The Magic of Psychotronic Power

Robert B. Stone

PARKER PUBLISHING COMPANY, INC.
West Nyack, N.Y.

Library of Congress Cataloging in Publication Data

Stone, Robert B
The magic of psychotronic power.

1. Success. 2. Occult sciences. I. Title.
BJ1611.2.S698 131'.32 77-14184
ISBN 0-13-545301-1

Printed in the United States of America

Dedication

When you work with your Psychotronic power and see your life improve you become faintly aware of cosmic forces at work outside of you in harmony with the power within you. To these forces, whoever, wherever, or whatever they are, I dedicate this book.

Other books by the author

Hypno-Cybernetics: Helping Yourself to a Rich New Life, S. Petrie with R. Stone

Power of Miracle Metaphysics

WHAT THIS BOOK CAN DO FOR YOU– AND HOW IT WORKS

Sai Baba is a holy man in India who can create material things out of thin air. "Are you God?" asked a young man.

"Yes. So are you," replied Sai Baba. "The only difference is: I know it."

Recently the great semanticist S. I. Hayakawa told about how he stopped smoking. He became aware that he was not enjoying the cigarettes. So he paid more and more attention to this fact. He began to realize he was really a nonsmoker. As this realization grew, the more miserable it became for him to light up. One day when he asked himself if he wanted a cigarette, he surprised himself by saying "no." He has been off cigarettes ever since.

The fire was started in the morning. The stones turned red hot by evening. Thousands gathered to see the Fiji fire-walkers perform.

The Fiji men chanted. They danced out on the hot stones in their bare feet. No burns.

What is the connection between a man who produces gems out of thin air, a man who stops smoking effortlessly, and men who walk on hot stones without injury?

All three are tapping psychotronic energy.

They may never have heard of it, but that does not matter. Turn a switch and the lights go on whether you heard of electricity or not.

Tapping this psychotronic energy is just as easy as turning a light switch. Most people have not heard about it. Although it has been around as long as man, and longer, scientists have only discovered it in the past five years and that is about as long as the name "psychotronics" has been in use.

Now this energy is under control. As you begin to use it, you get more and more incredible results. It is conceivable that you, too, could be using it to produce gems out of thin air, control your body, and walk on fire. But chances are you will want to start off with easier accomplishments, like:

- Kindle love for you in a formerly cold heart
- Double your income now and year after year
- Win at lotteries and gaming tables
- Correct disorders or diseases in your body and for others
- Become popular and "in demand"
- Solve problems in business with genius-like success
- Materialize a new car, new home, new job
- Turn personal weaknesses into herculean strengths
- Enjoy miraculous protection from harm
- Renew the cells of your body for longer life.

Psychotronic power has been eluding skeptics, so they continue to scoff. Meanwhile, it gets turned on for those who accept it. Miracles will happen for them until the skeptic arrives and says, "No." Then the miracles stop. Psychotronic power of the skeptic works, too. The way he wants it to work.

Belief is the "switch" to psychotronic power. Scientists learned this the hard way. For instance, they observed a person demonstrating how the energy of psychotronics could move an object across a table. But when they called in their skeptical colleagues, the demonstration failed. Psychotronic scientists now realize that their own consciousness affects their experiments.

These experiments now prove beyond a shadow of a doubt that once man turns on the psychotronic switch, he is connected to a vast Cosmic Psychotronic Generator that makes his every thought act just like it was a *fact*.

This book helps you to hook up to this Cosmic Psychotronic Generator. It then gives you systems for mentally creating benefits that become an accomplished fact in your life, sometimes before you are even finished reading the page. It literally puts immense power into your fingers and hands.

You learn how by pointing your fingers, or working certain patterns with your hands—"miracles" take place. These hand motions are triggering devices for the psychotronic energy of consciousness.

Your eyes are powerful emitters of this miraculous energy, too. You learn how by combining finger and eye technique. Nothing is impossible.

While psychologists study mental telepathy, while chemists check how the molecular structure of water is changed by a faith healer's hands, while doctors study mind affecting body through biofeedback, while physicists study levitation, materialization and dematerialization in the laboratory, you are able to use this energy today in your life.

You adjust your beliefs about what is possible or not possible.

You "hook in" to the Cosmic Psychotronic Generator.

You look.

You point your finger.

You exert god-like control over your life and your world.

Robert B. Stone

Acknowledgments

To the brave scientists who risked their professional reputations to examine a new energy, I tip my hat admiringly. May the International Association for Psychotronic Research continue to provide mankind with more and more knowledge about his energy of consciousness.

Regarding the effort that goes into putting a manuscript together, may I thank my wife Lola for her forbearance, my students for their contributions, and Mildred Christopherson for her dedication to the typewritten word.

Contents

1

THE KEY TO TURNING ON YOUR PSYCHOTRONIC POWER

You have a special power.

It is activated by an energy that scientists are just beginning to recognize and measure.

It is an amazing power. It works for you in ways that defy explanation. Scientists are watching this power in action under laboratory conditions—and wondering what is really going on.

This power seems to confirm fairy tales about the genie that appeared and assisted Aladdin whenever he rubbed his magic lamp; about the magic carpet that could fly its owner anywhere, instantly; and about the fairy godmother who arrived at just the right time to help with a crucial decision.

This power begins to work miracles for you as soon as you know you have it. It brings you money, love, health, and success. In what order? To what extent? You decide. The power carries out your decision, obeys your command.

Electricity did not begin to work for man until he knew it was there. Bring a native in from a remote jungle to a city and electricity will not work for him either until he realizes that this button turns on that light and that switch turns on this radio.

This power is called psychotronic power and this book explains your power to you and tells you how to push the buttons and turn the switches.

As you do, you get immediate proof that you have the power—just as immediate as the light guns on when you turn a switch.

You make things happen. You control your life. You enrich yourself and others. I have seen people use this power easily to:

- Make another person do their bidding
- Change an unfavorable decision even after it was made
- Magnify sexual appeal a hundred fold
- Inject harmony in place of hostility
- Cause painful disease symptoms to vanish
- Become a V.I.P.
- Acquire a new house or car or both.

When you use this power, it costs nothing. It does not get used up. It is always there, night and day.

I have found ways to concentrate and focus this power instantly, ways that make it act like a laser beam.

Sound complicated? Quite the contrary. It can be done with your fingers or through your eyes.

It is as simple as looking.

And . . . it is as simple as pointing your finger.

WHY PSYCHOTRONIC POWER MUST WORK FOR YOU

An unusual experiment was conducted in Czechoslavakia recently. A container, the dimensions of which are being kept secret, was stared into by one of the researchers. His "stare energy" was stored by this container. The container was then placed in another room. A wood pointer that could turn was attached to it. Four different fruits were placed under the pointer. Back in the first room, the researcher stared at a banana. In the next room, the pointer swung slowly to the banana. He stared at an apple. It swung to the apple. Every time the researcher stared at one of the four different kinds of fruits, his stare energy stored in a container in another room responded and turned the pointer to that fruit.

Here is the miraculous part of this experiment: If somebody else stared at the banana, the pointer would not respond. It seemed to know whose energy it was.

Your eyes and fingers produce a power that will work exclusively for you. In fact, it *is* yours and yours alone.

An American woman read how a Russian woman could move objects with her mind. It was done repeatedly in a laboratory with Russian scientists observing, measuring and recording. If a Russian woman could do it, certainly an American woman could do it, too, she reasoned. She practiced at first with aluminum foil. There were long hard hours of manipulating her thoughts, but nothing definite happened. Then she started staring at the aluminum foil and manipulating her fingers about a foot away from it.

It rippled. It moved!

A few months later, this woman was being observed and photographed moving aluminum foil, paper clips, and other small objects placed under a glass hood, by scientists.

These are interesting demonstrations of psychotronic energy and the power it can exert. But moving objects is a distortion of that power's real benefits. It is a nonmaterial power that intersects this material plane only slightly. It is somewhat like the iceberg. Ninety percent is below the surface.

Ninety percent of your psychotronic power operates in ways that do not produce heat, light or motion.

What does it produce? It produces necessities to man's survival through the laws of attraction and repulsion.

It works largely through intelligence and consciousness. It appears to cross great distances, penetrate walls, and span oceans. It is versatile.

Sarah L., 58, used her psychotronic energy to take years off her appearance and to radiate youth. Today she passes for twenty years younger.

Larry S. used his psychotronic energy to influence the roll of the dice, winning time after time.

David M. used his psychotronic energy to influence a business deal in his favor over one thousand miles away.

You point a finger for a few seconds.

You stare for a few seconds.

You make a miraculous change come about in your life. It is as if you rubbed your magic lamp and a genie did your bidding.

YOUR PSYCHOTRONIC GENERATOR AND HOW TO MAKE IT WORK FOR YOU

You have been already using your psychotronic power, but with very low voltage and therefore with only occasional results. You call it luck. Either things break for you or they don't, more often the latter.

There are ways to turn up the power of your psychotronic generator so that you get results every time.

The key to the psychotronic generator was discovered quite accidentally by two physicists. They were working with a spiritual healer whose psychotronic energy was being tested in the laboratory in many ways. They decided to use a cloud chamber to try to see the effects of her psychotronic energy.

A cloud chamber is a glass container filled with a gas that is ionized by cosmic energy entering the atmosphere. Sparks shoot downward within the chamber whenever cosmic rays hit it. Occasionally, a burst of cosmic energy causes a shower of these sparks.

This healer could cause a shower of sparks with her mind. She did it on signal from the scientists again and again. It was decided to try this at a distance. So they phoned her at home, seven hundred miles away. Again, at their signal, she caused the same flurry of sparks repeatedly. A week later, they tried again. This time they had several skeptical colleagues present to whom they wished to demonstrate this fantastic working psychotronic energy.

However, this time nothing happened. They checked the equipment, but found no flaws. Yet, as hard as she tried, the healer could cause no sparks in the cloud chamber. The skeptical scientists threw their hands up in a gesture of disgust and left.

The other two scientists knew what had happened:

Psychotronic power was working for the two skeptical scientists just as effectively as it was for the spiritual healer—maybe even more so, since they had two generators at work against her one generator. What they believed and expected to see turned on their psychotronic power to work in opposition to hers.

We are learning about this power in leaps and bounds. We know now how to block off an enemy's or a skeptic's psychotronic power so it does not interfere with ours.

We also know that the Czech could have stared at a picture of an apple just as effectively as an apple itself to activate the pointing needle to do likewise.

This means you can use a picture of a man or woman to exert your psychotronic power for control.

You can use a picture of a new house or a new car or a new boat to activate your receiving it.

You can even use a letter from another person or some belongings of that person, or even a hair off that person's head to make a "connection" so that your psychotronic power can flow to activate your bidding.

Roberta L. cooks with psychotronic energy! "Before I learned about mind power," she explains, "I was a terrible cook. I hated to prepare dinner. I burned every meal. You could pick up my fried eggs in your hand and eat them like toast."

Then she studied with the author and learned how to put psychotronic energy to work for her in the kitchen. "I felt the energy directing my hands. I began to enjoy my time in the kitchen. My family still can't believe the difference. They still ask, "Mom, did you cook this?"

Be it cooking, loving, succeeding–you can put your psychotronic energy to work for you.

The key to activating your psychotronic energy is *belief.* What you believe and can see defines the limits of your power.

The fact that you have this power and can work many miracles, health miracles, power miracles, and success miracles with it sounds incredible to you. But as you learn more about what scientists are discovering about this power on the pages ahead, your belief will be strengthened. This book will, in effect, be turning up the volume of your psychotronic power every page you turn. In just a chapter or two you will begin to see its miracles manifest in your life before your very eyes.

. . . And at your finger tips.

THE SPECIAL PHOTOGRAPHIC PROCESS THAT TAKES PICTURES OF YOUR PSYCHOTRONIC POWER

The psychic medium of yesteryear could perceive a mental body that seemed to surround the physical body. "The mental body is an object of great beauty, the delicacy and rapid motion of its particles giving it an aspect of living irridescent light," wrote Annie

Besant with Reverend C. W. Leadbeater at the start of this century. Theirs was a psychic view.

However, scientists a century ago were perceiving the same phenomenon. Human radiation or "effuvia" were observed as early as 1843 by Carsten in England. Nikola Tesla, the inventor of alternating current, began using a high voltage electric field to examine this radiation in the 1890's. But it took a Soviet husband-wife team, Semyon and Valentina Kirlian to perfect a photographic process using only photographic paper, no film, that captured this human radiation.

These photographs reveal flares and coronas around your body—especially your finger tips. If you are tired, there is less illumination. If you are angry, the colors are red. If you are in a prayerful mood, the colors are predominantly blue.

Dr. Don Parker, creator of SRA Reading Labs, has adapted the Kirlian method to study the reaction of one human aura on another. Fingers of a man and woman who touch change instantly. He calls his method psychophotography.

Jarbas Marinho, a civil engineer with the Brazilian Institute for Psychobiophysical research in Sao Paulo, has also produced Kirlian photography that shows energy transfer from person to person—psychotronic energy.

In the United States experiments reported at the Second World Psychotronic Conference in Monte Carlo, July, 1975, the emanations of a plant were successfully restricted by conscious action at a distance by two men and a woman each using his own consciousness, but in different ways.

What does it all mean? It means you can exert control over other people, if you know how to control your psychotronic power.

Let me tell you right here and now that learning to control your psychotronic power is easier than learning to ride a bicyle or learning to drive a car.

It is a natural ability. Man has always had this ability, but never really knowingly and purposely utilized it.

That time has come.

HOW SOME PEOPLE HAVE BEEN USING THEIR PSYCHOTRONIC POWER UNKNOWINGLY

In Claverham, England, there is an electrical engineer named Leonard Locker who uses a small nickel-plated pendulum attached to a string and held over a map to locate faults in underground electrical cables.

It was not until he retired as chief engineer for the South-Western Electricity Board in Bristol, England several years ago, that he started "dowsing" for cable breaks.

Now, companies all over England send him their cable maps when hard to locate breaks occur and he is uncannily accurate in pinpointing the trouble.

When Locker asks the pendulum to "point" to the break on a cable map, he is doing something not greatly different than the Czech who stared at the apple and his "stare" energy turned a pointer to an apple in the next room.

Both are using psychotronic power.

It is the same energy at work as when a dowser uses a forked stick and finds water when well-diggers failed.

The pendulum and dowsing rod work for everybody–when they become aware of psychotronic power. But then, as you will find on the pages ahead, once you do become aware of it, you can locate lost objects, discover mineral veins, and determine best locations for new enterprises, even without tools like the pendulum or dowsing rod.

Psychic healers, whether they use laying on of hands or prayer, are tapping psychotronic power.

You are going to learn to tap psychotronic power on the pages ahead, and you will be able to use it, as thousands are now doing for healing.

Psychic predictors, whether they are consciously aware of it or not, are using psychotronic power to transcend time and know the future.

When you learn to control your psychotronic powers, you will be able to predict events in the future.

Psychometry experts, like Peter Hurkos, who can touch an object involved in a crime and locate the criminal, are using their psychotronic power.

As you now become in control of your psychotronic power, you will be able to roll back time and span great distances to know what you want to know and accomplish whatever you want to have done.

Psychic powers, once the handmaiden of mysticism, are now becoming psychotronic power–

- Photographable
- Measurable
- Controllable

Your psychotronic power will become for you as miraculous as electricity appeared to be to your grandparents.

In fact, Dr. Shiuji Inomata of Japan's Electrotechnical Laboratory believes that the day will soon come when electrical energy will be converted into psychotronic energy. Computers will thus be given the abilities of human consciousness to see into the future and pick up information thousands of miles away.

YOUR FINGERS CONCENTRATE PSYCHOTRONIC ENERGY

Have you noticed how some people talk with their hands? As they speak to you, their hands keep emphasizing what they are saying with appropriate gestures and movements.

Hands are a channel for energy. We work with our hands, talk with our hands, explore with our hands. It is not only physical energy that is passed through our hands but psychotronic energy as well.

Since we learn from infancy with our hands, they are an especially appropriate starting point for learning to control psychotronic power.

You can probably see the psychotronic energy emanate from your fingertips, and you can probably feel it.

Action plan to sense psychotronic energy

To see it: Find a black background. Touch the fingertips of your left hand with the fingertips of your right hand. Take a deep breath and pull them slowly apart. You may see transparent white lines still connecting them.

To feel it: Hold your left palm vertically, facing right. Point the fingers of your right hand at your left palm. Keep the fingers at least six inches from your palm so you do not feel heat. Now slowly move your right fingers up and down as if you were shooting bullets at your left palm. As you do, you will feel a tingling or other sensation moving up and down your left palm. This is the feeling of your psychotronic energy.

To use it: Hold a picture of what you want to happen in your mind in a special way that I will teach you. Then point your fingers at the person or thing involved—or even just a picture or sketch of that person or thing—and what you want to happen has been activated.

Bill and Lillian S. knew just what kind of house they wanted. They did not have the fifty thousand dollars they knew it would take to build it, in fact, they were in debt. But they sketched the house–the floor layout and how it would look outside–and kept the plans where they could inject psychotronic energy into them with their fingers by touch and eyes by looking at them.

The small house they lived in was cramped. Day to day cash was always a problem. Nevertheless they knew they had created this from their original mental pictures having to do with "making a go of it" together. They were succeeding in that picture. Now they would succeed in their next picture.

Within months they were out of debt. Lillian received a large bequest of money and within another short period they had purchased land. One builder quoted seventy thousand dollars but they kept investing their plans with more psychotronic energy.

One day they met a builder socially. He studied the plans and bid thirty thousand. A bank readily agreed to finance it. Within six months, Bill and Lillian were living in their dream home paying less than the rent they were paying before.

Bill and Lillian lived in that house for fifteen years totally happy in it. But then they yearned for life in a tropical clime. They began to picture, plan, draw, and "program." You guessed it–that's where they are now.

YOUR EYES FOCUS PSYCHOTRONIC ENERGY

Did you ever stare at somebody and have them turn around and look at you?

A man who likes to look at pretty girls on the beach knows, even though a girl may not see him looking, she will adjust her bikini.

There is a power in the stare that you can feel just as easily as you feel power in your palm by pointing your fingers at it. Stare power that causes a person to turn, a girl to adjust her bathing suit, is the same power that the Czechs have learned to store in a specially shaped container and which will turn a pointer.

It is psychotronic power.

Adolph Hitler used that power against Czechoslovakia and other countries prior to the start of World War II. Witnesses who visited his private office in Berchtesgarten saw photographs of Prague, Warsaw, Antwerp, Amsterdam and other key European cities posted on the walls. Each photo had swastikas painted or pasted on them as if they were on the buildings in those photos.

Was he using some occult power when he gazed intently at these photos and willed what he saw to come true? Maybe he thought he was, but today science has de-occulted this process. It is the use of psychotronic power, or in this case, abuse.

Psychotronic power is no different than any other kind of power. Electricity can be used properly to advantage. Used improperly, it can electrocute. Heat can cook a meal and warm a house. It can also burn. Atomic power can run a generator, but it can also level a city.

Psychotronic power can bring you untold riches when used properly. But when used improperly, it, too, can bring pain and disaster—as Hitler came to know.

Read instructions before using, says the label. I place that label before you now. I promise on the pages ahead to not only give you the key to focus your psychotronic power for health, wealth, and success, but to do so safely, bringing abundant happiness to all involved in your use of it.

The eyes have it. The hands have it. Eyes and hands are psychotronic "guns."

You have stare power.

You have point power.

You have mental power that generates psychotronic energy which gets its "instructions" from your eyes and fingers to do your bidding like a giant slave.

HOW PSYCHOTRONIC POWER WORKS ITS MIRACLES

The definition of psychotronics at the beginning of this book describes how it is an interaction between consciousness and matter.

Scientists in all disciplines—physics, biology, medicine, chemistry—are now studying these effects of consciousness on the body and on the environment.

A waiter who could not afford a car to drive to work would stop each day in front of a beautiful house he passed while walking to work. How he would love to live in a house like that!

One evening, a woman he was serving in the restaurant said to him, "Young man, I have seen you looking at my house almost every day. I am going south to live, would you like to buy it?"

He explained how he had no such money. She explained how she would like to have the house to be in the hands of someone who would appreciate it and take care of it, even if it was no longer hers. She invited him to visit her. At that visit she agreed to sell him the house at a price so low he could pay it off out of his salary and tips. In a short while he was living in the house he had stared at.

On the fact of it, you could call this "coincidence." He just happened to like a house that was owned by a soft-hearted woman.

But then when you see psychotronic power at work bringing to the person that generates that power . . .

- A trip around the world
- A spouse
- A new lease on life
- A lost ring
- An executive position
- A court decision

. . . you begin to wonder if these are all really "coincidences."

Even scientists at work measuring and photographing psychotronic energy and seeing it perform "miracles" in the laboratory are not sure of the full nature of what they are dealing with.

Many are embarrassed at what the evidence points to. There appears to be a quality to space that permits psychotronic energy to go from here to there instantly. This does not conform with existing laws of physics as they are currently understood. It appears to be more within the scope of religion. People who use psychotronic power appear to exhibit god-like faculties. Naturally, scientists get somewhat shaken up by this, but they are persevering, especially in Communist countries where traditional religious concepts are not accepted.

It is just a matter of time before present laws of physics will be altered to accept the new data that psychotronics has supplied.

Meanwhile, it is easier to use psychotronic energy than to explain it.

Science has still not explained the sense of smell. The physical energies that radiate and cause fragrance to be emitted by a flower can only be surmised by science today. No measurement. No proof. Actually, there is more scientific proof of psychotronic energy than there is of the phenomenon we call "smell."

THE OLDEST POWER IN MAN'S HISTORY

The word "psychotronics" was only officially defined in 1975. But just as electricity was lighting up the sky as lightning long before the word electricity was born, so psychotronic energy has been affecting men's lives for millennia.

It was called "vital fluid" by medieval alchemists; "Mumia" by Paracelsus, the sixteenth century Swiss physician; "Animal Magnetism" by Mesmer, the Austrian doctor who pioneered in hypnotism around 1800; "Orgone Energy" by Wilhelm Reich; "Odic Force" by Baron von Reichenbach; and such different names by other scientists as "Vis Medicatrix Naturae," "Eloptic Energy," "Nervous Ether," "X-Force," and "Bio-Cosmic Energy."

Gurus of ancient India worked with a life energy they called "prana." They became adept at controlling this energy and in producing phenomena that astound scientists even today.

In Hawaii, where the author resides, the priests or kahunas worked with "mana." They could turn on this energy and improve the level of life and also bring about death. These secrets are emerging today.

Man has always had psychotronic energy, but he has not always turned it into power by harnessing that energy to do work.

We now know how to do this. The work that it can do for us is as unbelievable as the wireless telegraph was to our forebears, and radio, and television. We can control it.

When you learn to use your psychotronic energy on the pages ahead, you are learning to put this energy to work in ways that make television seem like child's play.

Energy at work is power. You will have the power to do things that only mystics and psychics have been able to do.

The reason they have been able to perform these "miracles" is that, knowingly or not, they have put their psychotronic energy to work.

The method is very simple. All it involves is your eyes, your thoughts, and occasionally your fingers. It gives you the secret "combination" to unlock sleeping abilities, such as the ability to:

- Predict future events
- Obtain the solution to a baffling problem
- Know where a person is and exactly what he is doing
- Be a "faith healer"

- Acquire a possession legally without money
- Affect the weather
- Locate oil wells, mineral veins and gems
- Cause a person to comply with your wishes.

What is more, you will be able to teach others these same fantastic things.

Georgette S. was admiring some pendants in a store. She saw one that seemed perfect for her. She invested it with her psychotronic energy in a special way. In a moment the owner of the shop came over to her, reached into the showcase, picked out that very pendant and handed it to Georgette.

"Like it?"

"I certainly do!"

"You may have it."

It was a gift. An unexplainable impulse experienced by the shop keeper.

Coincidence? Or psychotronics? (Remember what it means? ". . . The fields of interaction between people and their environment. . .")

FIRST STEPS IN HARNESSING YOUR PSYCHOTRONIC ENERGY TO DO YOUR BIDDING

Ben Franklin's electricity laboratory was a conversation piece among his neighbors. Weird jars, kites, metallic objects.

Your psychotronic laboratory is in a secret place, well-hidden from prying eyes and all set up with millions of dollars worth of generating and computorized equipment. It is located within your mind.

You already know how to use this fabulous organ of the human being. All that will be new in using it to generate psychotronic power to do special work for you is putting together certain attitudes, desires, and mental images in a special sequence and in a special way. What will also be new to you is adding laser-like focus with the help of your fingers and your eyes.

We all take our minds for granted. We don't use our mind consciously. It just happens.

You are reading now. You decided to open the book and read. You focus your eyes on the page. Reading happens.

Adding and other arithmetic chores require a little more "think power." Five and six are eleven. Seventeen and sixteen are (seven and six are thirteen, one and one are two carry one makes three–thirty three). It is mental work.

Using your psychotronic power is not mental work. It is easier than arithmetic. It is even easier than reading this book.

The reason it is so easy is it uses pictures instead of words and numbers.

Words and numbers are man-made devices. They differ from one country to another. But mental pictures are universal. A picture of a dog is a picture of a dog, whether in Kentucky or Kenya.

Pictures float in and out of our minds effortlessly, all day long. And much of the night. Dreams are mental pictures.

Psychotronic energy functions through mental pictures. You can command your psychotronic energy with the words, "I want a new gold Cadillac." But you will probably have a long wait ahead for you; if you ever get it.

On the other hand, if you use the mental picture of a gold Cadillac instead of the words, and use it together with your fingers in the special way you are about to learn, get the garage ready because that gold Cadillac is on the way!

THE FABULOUS BRAIN HAS VAST UNUSED POWER

"How can my brain, which has trouble adding and subtracting, produce a gold Cadillac?" you ask.

Let me tell you something about that brain of yours. It is composed of neurons which are something like electrical components in a radio or television set. There might be a hundred of these components in a television set, but do you know how many neurons in your brain?

Thirty billion.

The brain weighs only about three pounds–barely two percent of our body. Yet it contains thirty billion neurons capable of scanning for information and storing information.

Each neuron is composed of many atoms. All told there are one hundred trillion trillion atoms in the brain. That would be the number one with twenty-six zeros after it.

We are not used to thinking in such large numbers. This even goes many times beyond the national debt and other astronomical statistics.

Let's try translating one hundred trillion trillion into something more measurable. Suppose each atom was a BB pellet, about like the pellets used for an air gun. Now if you filled a living room with these pellets, it would use a lot of pellets. A hundred trillion trillion? Not quite. You would have to fill a living room every second for 94 million years to use them up.

Inconceivable? You bet it is! And yet most people dare to limit the human brain!

"It can't be done."

Oh, yes it can be done. And you are going to be doing it.

You are going to be using psychotronic power to save lives, create art and music, locate treasures, restore health, perform herculean tasks, sway opinion, and win at the game of life.

You can choose the path of the hero, the path of the saint, or the path of the sage.

That path can be a private country lane or public express freeway.

You will learn how to:

- Melt clouds or create rain
- See inside a person's body and correct what you see
- Command animals, birds, insects, and see them obey
- Sway a judge and jury when right is on your side
- Improve your own or somebody else's looks–complexion, radiance, demeanor
- Multiply business contacts and proliferate the influence of your firm
- Turn rivals into supporters
- Make prayers work
- Predict stock market changes
- "See" thousands of miles away.

And this is only the beginning. The above ten accomplishments may mean absolutely nothing to you. Your life style may entail different activities and have different needs.

Whatever your special needs are, your psychotronic power stands ready to deliver them.

Are you ready to push the button?

2

USE YOUR PSYCHOTRONIC POWER TO MAKE YOUR WISHES COME TRUE

You begin to see visible effects of your psychotronic energy by making plants grow faster. Armed with this confidence, you are able to attract the opposite sex to your side with mental commands and psychotronic hand motions. You learn to get information about a person from an object that belongs to that person, and to detect information a distance away that you could not possibly know otherwise. Finally, you see how to change circumstances that you do not want to happen.

Let's get down to business,–the business of harnessing psychotronic power to do your bidding.

Is there somebody you like very much and who you wish would like you more? You are going to make that wish come true in the next few minutes, and you will not have to leave the chair you are sitting in.

I am going to give you a very simple procedure to begin with. We must crawl before we walk. This procedure, as simple as it is, is still effective. You will see it work. It will probably work within twenty-four hours, certainly within seventy-two.

How do you turn on psychotronic power? No switch, no rheostat, no faucet. But it is something like all three.

Can you imagine a bright red apple? Can you imagine taking a bite out of it and now seeing the inside where you bit into it?

If you had a specific apple in mind, and if you had an electronic device similar to the brain encephalograph connected to that apple in the proper way, that apple would react the moment you thought of biting into it.

Cleve Backster who discovered that simple lie detector equipment—the polygraph—could record plants reacting to human thought, also worked with chicken eggs. With each egg of a dozen hooked up to its separate polygraph and meter, all of the meters would react to his decision to eat an egg for breakfast. When he opened the refrigerator door and reached for the first egg, eleven meters stopped agitating and the one he was reaching for became even more agitated.

We should not jump at the conclusion that the egg was getting a nervous breakdown. It could have been excited over fulfilling a high purpose or destiny—being eaten by man.

The important thing is the egg "knew." The imaged thought that Backster had, "I'll eat this egg," was transmitted.

What you will be thinking in a moment will be transmitted, too, but in an even more powerful way.

THE FIRST STEP IN EFFECTIVE PSYCHOTRONIC POWER TRANSMISSION

An instructor is teaching a course that leads to greater awareness and ESP. It is called Silva Mind Control. Students have been asked to relax and visualize their pet cat or dog or a neighbor's pet. They work with this pet by lifting it up in their imagination, turning it around, and viewing it from several vantage points.

The next day when students return for their next class, a discussion almost always arises about how more affectionate their pet was that evening.

Picturing in the mind is the "faucet" that turns on psychotronic energy.

Try it out yourself before using it on a person. If you do not have a pet cat or dog, do it on plants. Here is a way to do it with mung bean sprouts.

Action plan

Soak mung beans overnight. Separate them in the morning into two identical glasses, one on the left, one on the right. Water each exactly the same. However, several times a day, wherever you may happen to be . . .

Visualize the right hand glass. Send kind thoughts to this batch of mung beans. Ignore the left hand batch. While doing this . . .

Imagine you are giving extra water to the right hand glass. Use your hands to go through the motion of watering.

See the difference within two or three days. The mung beans in the right hand glass will thrive on your psychotronic energy compared to those in the left hand glass.

We have been told by our parents and then our teachers that our imagination is a useless thing. "It's *just* your imagination." How many times have we said that to somebody, or heard it said to us.

Well, I have some interesting news for you. Scientists now realize the imagination is the key to getting things done. If it does not happen in somebody's thoughts first, it does not happen period.

Imagination is the "faucet" that turns on psychotronic power.

A jeweler uses it when he designs a new ring, "seeing" it, sketching it, then producing it.

An architect uses it when he designs a building, "seeing" it, sketching it, rendering it; then having it converted into working drawings, specifications, blueprints, and then built.

A fiction writer uses it to create his characters. He "sees" them, lives with them in his imagination. A book is created.

The more realistically you can imagine, the more that psychotronic "faucet" is turned on.

HOW TO ATTRACT A PERSON TO YOUR SIDE

If you have proved to your satisfaction that your imagination can "contact" a pet or make sprouts grow faster, you are ahead of the person who just says "maybe."

What you *know* is what works for you.

In Poland, medical researchers studied why some medicine worked well when prescribed by certain doctors, but hardly worked at all when prescribed by other doctors.

They found that the expectation of the doctors was influencing the results. Doctor A accepted the new medicine, prescribed it, and was happy with the improvements it brought about. He continued to use it successfully.

Doctor B was skeptical when he first used the new medicine. He did not expect a positive result when he prescribed it. The results bore out his doubtful expectations. If he prescribed it again, he did so knowing again it would probably not work. It didn't.

Consciousness affects matter–even the "automatic" action of a chemical on the body.

Your consciousness is going to affect another body now–the body of somebody you wish to attract to your side.

If you don't think it can be done, you are right.

If you do think it can be done, you are also right.

You had better prepare yourself mentally for a positive result. Examine any doubts you may have. Are the doubts more important to you than anything else? The hang on to them. And keep the faucet of your psychotronic power shut.

On the other hand, if you have a "gut" feeling that mankind is now discovering more about his own consciousness, that there has been at least some truth to the many instances of the power of thinking positively, working "miracles," and that everybody is endowed with more mental power than he is using, then you are able to open the "faucet" of your psychotronic power with your visual imagination.

Arthur L. was bashful. He did not date girls until several years after his friends had started going out. Now he had dated one girl but was afraid of calling her again for fear of being refused. He knew where she worked and would often pass by and look in just to catch a glimpse of her. He asked me to help him arrange a chance meeting with psychotronic power. He visualized himself meeting her, shaking hands, talking with her using his hands. He admitted he felt nervous talking to her even in his imagination.

Two days later nothing had happened. So he parked his car and started toward her shop to get another "stolen" glimpse of her, when all of a sudden there she was walking towards him. It caught him by surprise. He became flustered. All he could do was stammer out a hello and keep walking.

Psychotronic power had worked perfectly for him. It brought him back exactly what he had put into it.

Remember the story about the man who wanted to catch a mouse that he knew was in his house? He had a mousetrap but no cheese to bait it with. So he used a magazine picture of cheese. In the morning there in the trap was a picture of a mouse.

Moral: you get out what you put in.

Arthur L. gained nothing by the incident, except the realization that he had bigger and better work to do. He went back to the "drawing board" and again saw his girl friend and him together. This time he made sure he felt at ease and confident while in this mental posture. He met her again. It was a better meeting. He met other girls. Each meeting became better and better.

Put in expectation of results and you get results. Put in visual images that are realistic and these images become real. Put in acceptance of your psychotronic power and you enjoy the "miracles" of that power.

Now you know what I mean when I say, "Are you ready?"

Are you? Then let's do it.

Action plan to attract a person to your side

Relax so you can use your imagination in a comfortable day-dreaming way. Close your eyes.

See the person you wish to attract to your side. That person is doing something typical–smoking, combing hair, working.

Talk to the person, mentally. See the person look up and respond with a smile. Keep this talk going for about a minute. Small talk at first, health, weather, then talk about the two of you. Emphasize your loving thoughts (even if an opponent or enemy). Talk about your respect and high esteem for that person.

Use your hands in some way, either to emphasize your point, to hold hands, or to stroke the person if that fits into the relationship.

End your psychotronic session by feeling it openended. Feel as if there has been only an interruption and that the "conversation" will soon be continued. Open your eyes.

HOW YOUR HANDS HELP TO POWER YOUR PSYCHOTRONIC ENERGY

The meeting you have just daydreamed about has been activated just as surely as the blueprint activates the house.

The mental picture is like the television camera capturing a scene. It then is transmitted out into space, where it finds television sets tuned into its wavelength. That picture then appears on a screen of those sets.

The person in your "Action Plan" may not understand why. But you enter their thoughts. The words you uttered may not be detected consciously but the feeling behind those words–a warm, loving feeling–will probably be detected consciously. The reaction you expected will then be triggered.

Sometimes, the other person tunes you out, but "coincidence" takes over. Chance seems to be at work. The meeting still takes place, as if there was a "mind" bigger than the two of you that "arranged" it.

One day we will know exactly how psychotronic energy works. Meanwhile, we can only conjecture–while we put it to good use.

Roberta L. lost a wallet. Several days passed without her being able to locate it. She called me and asked how she could locate her wallet. Then she followed my instructions. She relaxed, closed her eyes, and visualized a clock showing 10 o'clock, and a calendar showing that same day's date. "Tonight at 10, I will know where my wallet is!" Exactly at 10 that night, she got a phone call from her boyfriend. "I found your wallet in my car," he reported.

The next day she called me and told me what had happened. "I still don't have my wallet," she sulked. I reminded her that the problem was locating it and now that problem was solved. "You know how to solve the current problem." She hung up. Then she phoned me the next day. "I mentally gave him 24 hours to bring it back," she complained, "and he was one hour late." This time I hung up.

Are the neurons of our brain in tune with the neurons of other brains and able to pick up information and transmit it? Or, is our brain part of a bigger Universal Intelligence? Perhaps neither theory is exactly right. But we can transcend the boundaries of our skull. And we are not alone doing this. Plants do it. Animals do it. Even single cells do it.

What we need to address ourselves to, rather than to theory, is to the way to make this energy work for us in bigger and better ways and under more perfect control.

Relax. Visualize. What else? The hands are one more way to induce bigger and better benefits and to do so with more perfect control.

Kirlian photography has shown powerful energy radiating from the fingertips. This energy intersects the physical plane only slightly. Use it to move objects across a table and it may take you hours to get just a slight movement.

But this energy operates on a plane that is more important than physical energy and physical work. It is the energy of life itself, generated by consciousness, able to do its real work on the plane of consciousness.

So when you use your hands to direct psychotronic energy to people, you are in its modality, its kingdom, its sphere of influence.

Relax, visualize, and point.

That begins to activate psychotronic power to win you the benefits you seek.

Point at what? Point at a map, a portrait, an object belonging to the person.

Ralph A. had courted Lillian S. for several years. She was his dream girl. Now they were going to be married. Then suddenly she left him for another man. He was stunned. His dreams turned into a nightmare. Now she was a thousand miles away.

She had left a scarf behind. He decided to use it in a special way, applying the laws of psychotronic energy.

He held the scarf in his hand as he relaxed comfortably in a chair. He imagined he saw her. He pretended that he was offering her the scarf. He extended it to her. When she reached for it in his imagination, he gently pulled her to him—mentally. Within three weeks she returned to him and later they were married.

The hands are not essential to psychotronic communication, but they reinforce it.

We will go into techniques to make the hands manipulate our psychotronic energy in a later chapter. Meanwhile, look at your hands. They have been an ingenious tool for you. No other living creature has been endowed with hands which work anywhere near as well. They make civilized life possible for you. Now see in your hands another ability which will improve your level of life even more—magnifier of psychotronic power.

HOW EYES AND HANDS TOGETHER HELP TO POWER PSYCHOTRONIC ENERGY

Eastern philosophy has always been considered as nonscientific. But it has accepted long before western philosophers the existence of a close connection between man and the universe in a conscious sense. In yoga, the individual's mind is considered as an extension of Universal Mind.

It is seen as an outcropping, pretty much as flowers burst out on a tree. So the yogi sees himself as potentially capable of exhibiting all of the faculties of Universal Mind, being part of it. All he needs to do is erase the illusion of separation from Universal Mind and join more with it. Hence the word Yoga, meaning yoke or joining.

By training the body and mind, the yogi (man) or yogini (woman) is able to be all, know all, do all, because all of the Universal Mind is activated by the yogic mind.

The yogi uses his arms, hands, feet, eyes, backbone, breath and mind to join with Universal Mind. Advanced yogis attain control over their body and mind that permits them to consciously feel one with the Universal Mind.

We see in modern western approaches to applying psychotronic power several similarities to what yoga has taught for centuries—the relaxation, the mental attunement and picturing, the expanding of the self-image. But we also see some important differences, and we consider these differences to be a step forward.

In the west, the energy concept gives us a set of reference points that fits into our scientific approach, an approach that has brought us to where we are today. The energy is seen concentrated in the eyes and hands. So we use the eyes and the hands as "appliances" in converting psychotronic energy into practical benefits.

We may be missing something by bypassing the disciplines inherent in Eastern ways. We may be "storming the gates of Heaven" and using an energy for practical benefits before we have purified our consciousnesses so as to have the wisdom to use it properly.

Atomic energy raises the same question. Are we ready to use that energy or are we like children playing with matches?

I and other psychotronic "engineers" have wrestled with this concept as I suppose did the scientists who harnessed the energy of the atom. Personally I am convinced that the time has come for man's next step. Everything is accelerating. Those who do not learn to use their psychotronic power to contribute to their own and general human betterment may be left behind.

You view generators and power lines creating and distributing electrical energy quietly and easily. You see the wires bringing this power silently into your home. Begin to look at yourself as such a system. See your conscious awareness as a natural, easy generator, your hands and eyes as quiet transmitters of this energy.

You have seen electronic miracles take place. Now expect psychotronic miracles.

HOW TO GET THE ANSWER YOU NEED

The first International Conference on Psychotronics took place in Prague in 1973. The assembled scientists shared their research in measuring and using psychotronic energy. Besides Kirlian photography of this energy, there was a great deal of work shared in the field of radionics. This covers getting information as by dowsing, by psychometry (holding an object), and by a controversial apparatus that several scientists had devised.

One woman who had such a radionics device commonly called a black box was able to accomplish without it the same detection of information which she claimed it could do for her. Francis Farrelly was given a piece of mineral rock by a professor from the Czechoslovak Academy of Scientists; he asked her to identify its origin and age.

Using her hands and eyes for a few moments she then stated that the rock came from a meteor and was 3.2 million years old. This was exactly the opinion of Czech experts who had analyzed it.

Try this parlor game on your friends: Pass around a paper bag. Ask them to drop into it a ring, watch, comb or other belonging so that nobody can see. Then pass the bag around again. Have everyone take out an object not his own. As soon as they have it in their hands and without examining it for clues, ask them to describe the person that owns it by describing their own feelings while holding the object.

The results are often quite dramatic. The hands are radionic sensors of the body and can pick up information. This information is usually shrugged off as unreliable, if indeed we are at all conscious of it.

Now your guests are conscious of it and will offer such comments as:

"This person is very insecure."

"A female, quite energetic."

"A very sad person suffering some loss."

The owners of the object will likely confirm most of the information offered.

If anybody can do this, can you imagine how much better you can do it, knowing how?

Action plan to get information from an object

Hold an object connected to the person or project about which you wish information.

Wrap the fingers of one hand around it as you gaze intently at your hand.

Ask the question you wish to have answered. Do so mentally.

Close your eyes and wait for the answer.

Be aware of how you feel, what you "see" or "hear."

Accept thoughts that come apparently out of the blue.

Here are the kinds of questions you can ask about a person:

- Where is this person now?
- What is this person doing now?
- How does this person feel now?

Or, you can ask these questions about a business or a project:

- Is this the right time?
- Is this the right place?
- Will this succeed?

Famous psychic Peter Hurkos has been able to describe vivid scenes of a crime taking place by holding some object involved. He has helped police solve murders.

Everybody walks, reads, breathes, eats. But nobody holds an object in his hand to get information. So we do not think it can be done. But it can be done. And those who accept the fact that it is worth trying, are able to do it.

Dowsers do it in a special way to get specific information about locating water. The stick or rod merely accentuates the radionic sensing of the (substitute) hands.

HE FOUND THE STOLEN MONEY BAG FOR POLICE

Recently a robbery took place in Boulder Creek, California. The gunman was captured by police after a chase on foot, but along the way he had hidden the loot—a money bag containing $2500 in cash. After a four-hour fruitless search by police and citizens, someone remembered there was a psychic who lived in town, Christopher Hills. Why not have him help?

The deputy sheriff of Santa Cruz, figuring there was nothing to lose, agreed. So did Hills. He got his dowsing rod made of the bones of a male and female whale. Starting at a point between where the robbery occurred and where the gunman was captured, and holding the separate prongs of the divining stick between the fingers in each hand, he slowly rotated his body. The stick resisted being turned at a certain point.

Hills headed off in that direction. The stick apparently pulling him along. It was across rough terrain, over fences and through thickets, with police and citizens hard put to keep up with him. Then he fairly dived into some bushes and came up with the money bag—elapsed time: five minutes.

I have known Christopher Hills for many years. We have written more than one book together. He is a pioneer in the study of the energy that surrounds matter and the conductivity of intelligence through space. What he is able to do, others can do, and he teaches the philosophy and its practical application at his University of the Trees in Boulder Creek.

You are now learning the philosophy and practical use of this psychotronic energy. Whether you use a dowsing rod, a pendulum, or some other device, or whether you just permit your hands and mind to work together without these tools does not really matter.

You *can* detect information which you seek to know.

HOW TO TUNE YOUR PSYCHOTRONIC ENERGY DETECTOR TO THE PRECISE INFORMATION YOU NEED

When you desire to eat, your mind resonates to food. You are in tune with food sources.

When you desire to make love, your mind resonates with the opposite sex. You become finely tuned to your opportunities.

When you desire information about a particular project or problem, your mind resonates with it. You become tuned in to what you need to know.

Thomas Edison was a great inventor because he knew this, was aware of the information–or, if you prefer, intuitive "flashes"–that he was about to receive, and trusted them.

George Washington Carver trusted his "conversations" with the peanut vines and came up with use after use. Botanist Luther Burbank had a similar affinity for fruit trees and appeared to be guided by them in creating new hybrid fruits.

Is there some information you want to know right now?

Do you consider you have a right to it and that it will help you without hurting others?

Do you trust the human mind's ability to intuitively perceive beyond the limits of sight, sound, etc.?

Can you conceive of a person or thing connected with this information, as if you were there?

If your answers are "yes" to these four questions, you are ready to perform an information acquiring feat that would stun Sherlock Holmes.

The weakest of your four "yes" responses is probably the third "yes." We have been taught to trust only our sensory information. We trust what we see, hear, touch, smell and taste.

When Jose Silva, founder of Silva Mind Control, began teaching his own children in so-called subjective learning, he tested them and found they would volunteer information or answers before he could ask the question.

"Why did you answer that question?" he asked.

"I guessed you wanted to know," was the reply.

I myself have trained children in this ability and have found they are more readily able to accept psychic functioning than are adults. One eight-year-old did not even have to relax and close her eyes, as I am going to have you do in a moment. She just came up with accurate answers about people she did not know again and again by just "guessing."

Children have less "I can't" training than do adults. The older we get, the further we drift from that natural, intuitive perception with which we are all endowed. Corporation executives who have retained their trust in hunches have been found to be more successful than those who ignore the still, small voice of intuition and rely instead on statistical reports.

In a moment, you are going to get a "hunch." It will not be delivered to your consciousness any differently than other thoughts you have. Expect it. And expect it to be dependable.

Decide on the information you need to acquire and you can begin.

SEVEN SIMPLE STEPS TO ACQUIRE INFORMATION MILES AWAY

Action plan to get information at a distance

Sit in a comfortable chair. Close your eyes. Take a deep breath and relax.

Turn your eyes slightly upward as if in thought.

Mentally ask for the information you seek.

Visualize the scene involved.

Use your hands to emphasize your seeking. Pretend you are psychometrizing a book, record, or other object, if such is involved, or pretend you are gesturing with your hands if another person is involved.

Stop visualizing the scene.

Guess at the information you need–accept the answers that come.

You improve with practice. Start with projects that are less vital. As you receive verification of your accuracy, move on to more critical information.

Here are some examples of the kind of information you can acquire. These examples are arranged in order of increasing importance. You would want to start with the less important type of matters that head the list, working your way down the list as your psychotronic "attunement" proves its accuracy.

- Is that movie still playing at the neighborhood theatre?
- Is the sequence of that television show a repeat and have I seen it already?
- Will_________ be on time?
- What will the weather be like tomorrow?
- What does _________ think of me?
- What mark have I been given on that test?
- What mark has _________ been given on that test?
- What company needs my services?
- Who is responsible for _________?
- When is the check being mailed to me?

- Who is that person with right now?
- Should I buy or sell?
- What does ________ want most?
- Where should I go for ________?
- What should I guard against most from my competition?
- What is in that letter, document or report?

PSYCHOTRONIC ENERGY FLOWS BOTH WAYS–YOU CAN NOT ONLY DETECT BUT ALSO CORRECT

George D. wanted to divide his property. Officials said it could not be done. Agricultural land had to be preserved in this area and it was feared that further subdivisions would encourage housing and discourage farming.

A year before, George would have visualized himself hassling with the authorities. He would have worried himself sick and, in the process, used his energy of consciousness to create the very outcome he feared. But now, knowing the power of his psychotronic energy, George sketched his property on a piece of paper. He then made a light line where the subdivision would be, as it was already shown on the survey submitted with his subdivision application.

Daily he held the sketch in his hand and went over the line making it stronger each time. He closed his eyes and saw the officials looking at the survey. He "spoke" to them of his need and its reasonableness.

In a few weeks, the officials reversed themselves and he got his approval.

Need and reasonableness, free of any thoughts of failure, are the keys that permitted George's psychotronic energy to work fast and successfully. Instead of creating the problem, he created the solution.

It is as if a larger intelligence is involved and which mediates. Not who is right, but what is right. But the larger intelligence needs your agreement and cooperation.

Your psychotronic power can correct an injustice being done to you or somebody else, a lot easier and more successfully than it can be used to create an injustice. To do wrong with psychotronic power is up hill all the way and you never know what can come back rolling down the hill at you to correct the wrong. Psychotronic power works both ways.

Evelyn L. was a prominent real estate agent in her rural area. People respected her advice. Now she was in trouble. The courts had overturned a requirement in a contract of sale requiring that only new houses be built. The buyer was going to bring in a second hand cottage from a mile down the road.

"What will I tell the other buyers? They have hired architects. Their new house will be downgraded by his eyesore." She was on the verge of tears. I gave her instructions. She had been waking up in the middle of the night, visualizing a shack on that property and tormenting herself. Now when she woke up and "saw" that shack, she used her hands to put an "x" through it and then "saw" a beautifully landscaped house.

One night when she awoke, she heard a noise across the street from her bedroom, where the property was located. There was the roar of a motor truck and the commotion of men shouting. She got up to look. The movers had arrived with the second-hand house, and the ramshackled thing was being unloaded. All of a sudden there was a crash. The house had collapsed.

She went back to sleep.

A few months later, a new, landscaped house was built on that property.

Evelyn did not use her psychotronic power to destroy the second hand structure. She merely "saw" the situation as it should be.

Previously she had been "seeing" the problem. Now, instead, she "saw" the solution. Had she not switched from worrying about the shack and "seeing" the problem, her psychotronic energy would help to create the unwanted condition.

When she used her hands to put an "x" through the shack, she was not determining just how the problem would be corrected. She left that to the larger intelligence through which our personal psychotronic power seems to work.

In the chapters ahead we will work with proven techniques that convert problems into solutions using the miraculous power of our psychotronic energy.

The mind, the eyes, and the hands will be all we need to work these "miracles." With them we will correct injustices, avoid unwanted circumstances, improve situations. We detect information and then use that information to create a better life for ourselves and our loved ones.

3

HOOK UP WITH THE COSMIC PSYCHOTRONIC GENERATOR FOR UNLIMITED POWER OVER OTHERS

In this chapter you learn to amplify your psychotronic energy many fold for unlimited power. You are able to sway a person to your way of thinking without saying a word. You can melt clouds. Now the world becomes yours. You have it in the palm of your hands as you set goals, give them priority, and reach them one by one.

You have psychotronic energy. It is your life energy—the energy of your consciousness and aliveness.

As you dull your consciousness or detract from your aliveness, your psychotronic energy diminishes.

Laboratory photographs of this energy show that sick people have dimmer "auras" and their energy does not radiate out as far from their body as it does when they are healthy.

Both physical illness and mental illness affect the radiated "aura". Its color changes. Its intensity changes.

When a spiritual healer uses the laying on of hands to help another person, Kirlian photography shows that the healer's hands lose some of their psychotronic energy which the person he helped gains in psychotronic energy.

We need to keep our body well fed with "alive" foods. This means natural foods not depleted of their minerals and vitamins. We need to eat whole wheat bread, not white bread, brown rice, not white rice, fresh produce instead of packaged or canned, and some raw fruits and salads every day.

We need to keep our body clean, exercised, and rested. We need to keep it as free as possible of smoke, alcohol, stimulants, medicines–including aspirin and sleeping pills.

We need to keep our mind free of negative thoughts and attitudes that act the same way as pollutants do in our body. We need to resolve differences rather than to permit them to fester as resentment or hostility. We need to observe our own reactions and avoid deceit and dishonesty.

With a solid foundation of a healthy body and mind, our psychotronic energy is generated in powerful amounts–powerful enough to see us through any common situations, emerging victorious and successful.

It is as if we had a psychotronic generator that works best when we keep all parts in repair, clean and well lubricated.

But just as we have a mind that occasionally seems to exhibit characteristics of being part of something bigger–like a Universal Mind or Infinite Intelligence–so our own private psychotronic generator seems to be connected to something bigger than it is.

Let's call this bigger source of power a Cosmic Psychotronic Generator, for that indeed is the way it behaves.

WHY HOOKING UP YOUR PSYCHOTRONIC GENERATOR TO THE COSMIC PSYCHOTRONIC GENERATOR CREATES UNLIMITED POWER

As scientists begin to understand consciousness they see it as the creative force in the universe–as well as the destructive force in the universe.

As they delve into its energetic characteristics they begin to see it as creating laws of the universe as well as obeying these laws.

It is as if whatever is behind the creation of the universe is still at work partially through man's mind.

Some years ago, in accepting a Nobel prize for discovering a sub-atomic particle, a physicist publicly commented, "I wonder if that particle was there before I started looking for it."

Man is certainly aware of the fact that he is creating his part of the universe. What he is not aware of is that his mind is related to *the* creative force behind the universe itself.

Strange things happen when he does become aware of this relationship. He begins to display god-like abilities. He is able to affect matter, go forward and backward in time, span any distance through thought . . . . and control people.

Most religions separate man, as a creator, from the Universal Creator. Man is not God. When Sai Baba told the young man, "Yes, I am God, and so are you, the only difference is, I know it," he was really saying that he was within God and God was within him. He was not trying to give the impression that he was God come to visit earth. He was saying, "What I can do, you can do, if you were to become aware of your full capability."

"Hooking up" is acquiring this awareness. If you are now feeling comfortable with the last page or two, you are getting "hooked up." On the other hand, if previous concepts taught at home, religious school, or college are interfering with an unlimited concept of yourself, you need to study some of the work science is doing in the field of consciousness.

Science is discovering man's god-like abilities. It is working with these abilities in the laboratory. It is finding that when man does two things with his mind, some fantastic changes take place. Those two things are:

1. Relax body and quiet thoughts
2. Be aware of being part of the Universe.

Some will recognize these two steps as the fundamentals of meditation. But don't get hung up on words. God. Meditation. Religion. Prayer. Science is creating new words for what has up until now been in the domain of religion.

Trespass? Never the two shall meet? That's what I meant when I said man separates himself from God. The choice is really a personal one. You can see the god in yourself–or not.

Florence G. did. She was a common-law wife at the age of 17, twice a mother by 19. At 20 she left her two boys with her own mother in Connecticut and roamed the country. On the West Coast years later, she was a drifter, selling door-to-door occasionally to make money, and acquiring a temporary husband and two more permanent children.

She happened to meet another young woman who got her interested in yoga, meditation, astrology, and psychic functioning. She was introduced to my classes in awareness expansion. Within two years she was happily married, a successful yoga teacher, commercial artist, and dance instructor, appearing on television and manifesting in her life everything she ever wanted–including a renewed relationship with her now teen-aged Connecticut sons.

Florence is aware of what she was doing. She is aware that she has the ability to create her own life. She decides, pictures, realizes. The people she comes into contact with now see her quite differently than those she knew in "drifter" days. She is respected, sought after for advice and surrounded by friends.

Call it what you will, but when you relax and turn your awareness to the universe of which you are part, you get "hooked up" to your god-like powers.

HOW TO GET "HOOKED UP" IN TWO MINUTES

Your psychotronic generator is naturally "hooked up" with the Cosmic Psychotronic Generator. We have the freedom to unhook ourselves and most of us have taken that route. Our stomach needs to be fed. Our body needs to be sheltered.

There is a woman who took that path of "me first." As middle age approached she realized life was passing her by and, even though she had a family and all the comforts she needed, something was missing. She decided to give up everything that separated her from all people, including her own name and identity. She gave away all of her possessions, called herself Peace Pilgrim and decided to dedicate herself to the unity of all mankind.

Today she has walked many tens of thousands of miles dressed in her tunic and carrying only a toothbrush and comb, never any money. Wherever she goes she brings joy and happiness. She was arrested for vagrancy in Washington, D.C. and put in jail. When they came to get her in the morning, she had all the prisoners singing and they did not want her to leave. She is today a happy person never wanting for food or friends or a comfortable place to sleep wherever she roams.

This is not to say that you have to give up your life, start a new one, in order to get "hooked up."

But you do have to give up part of it: two minutes.

Are you willing to trade that two minutes for what scientists are finding it produces?

- Extra energy all day long
- Relief from anxiety, worry, depression
- More outgoing, attractive personality
- Better perception
- Peace of mind
- Lowered blood pressure
- Less desire for stimulants or tranquilizers
- Fewer, if any, headaches
- Reduction of over-eating.

What scientists are not quite ready to put into words yet are the less measurable but more dramatic changes that place in

- Control over other people
- Control over wealth
- Control over health
- Control over life destiny.

The price: two minutes. Are you ready to pay it? Then you are ready to begin.

Action plan to hook up your psychotronic generator to the cosmic psychotronic generator

Close your eyes and turn them slightly upward.

Create a room in your imagination. Walls, floor, ceiling, windows. Paint this room any colors you wish, decorate, carpet, furnish.

Install a large skylight in this room. Place a chair under the skylight. The chair you will use every time you visit this room. It is bathed in light from the sky.

Sit in this chair mentally now. Feel the light on you as a golden glow.

Understand this universal light to be like a handshake with your own light within.

Stay this way for about a minute, feeling love for the universe, aware of its vastness and intelligence, of being part of it, of your being.

Resolve to enjoy this minute again soon.

Open your eyes.

Many techniques are being used today to teach people to take that step forward in consciousness which science has taken a new interest in. The technique of creating a special "room" in the consciousness may one day be replaced with some other more effective way, but meanwhile this way works. It works wonders and it has been used by Inner Peace Movement, Silva Mind Control, Mind Dynamics, and other training systems.

What matters more than technique is intention.

DEFINE YOUR INTENTION AND YOU FLIP THE SWITCH

Arthur M. Young, inventor of the world's first commercial and licensed helicopter, has long been interested in the scientific study of consciousness as a basic ingredient of the universe. He has looked into various devices that psychics use, including the "black box" mentioned in the previous chapter. He concluded that such devices were merely assisting the consciousness to tune in or concentrate.

Intention, states Young, is the key. Desiring to diagnose a disease permits the mind to tune in to a patient's condition. The devices are just a catalyst for the mental process.

Jose Silva, founder of Silva Mind Control, agrees. He sees desire to know the answer to a problem creating a resonance with that problem and everything connected with it.

Your intention right at this very moment is already attuning your mind. But what good is a radio set all tuned in to a station, if it is not plugged in, or turned on.

Go back to the room you just created. Get plugged in and turned on so your psychotronic generator, reinforced by the Cosmic Psychic Generator can begin to work for you.

Sit under the skylight in your imagination whenever you go to your special room. Oliver Wendell Holmes once defined inspired thinking as belonging not to the one-story intellects, or two-story intellects, but to the three-story intellects "with skylights."

One-story intellects, he said, are merely fact collectors. Is that all you want to be?

Two-story intellects, he said, use the facts collected by fact collectors and add their own reason and logic. This is better, but you can be much more.

You can be a three-story man with a skylight. These men, he said, imagine, idealize, and predict. They are illumined men, he said–enlightened by the skylight.

USING "INTENT" TO CLOSE THE POWER CIRCUITS

The process of getting plugged in to psychotronic energy on a Cosmic level and turning it on to do your bidding, is the easiest process ever devised. No elaborate procedures, no three-step method, no complicated directions to follow.

It just takes intent.

What this means is that by wishing it to happen–it will happen. This is the lesson behind all the legends and fairy tales that have survived through the centuries. The reason they have survived is that people have a subliminal acceptance of them. Mind knows what mind is and what mind can do. This knowing may not be conscious but it is nevertheless there.

You are now facing a critical minute in your life. If you are ready to assume more control over your life–your success, your health, your influence over others–you need to affirm to yourself that this is indeed your intent.

Make this affirmation your special room.

Action plan to energize psychotronic power through intent

Go to your "special room" again by closing your eyes and imagining yourself there.

Review the furnishings, color scheme and other familiar aspects of it.

Sit in the special chair, again feeling the warm embrace of the universal light.

State mentally your intent to take more control of your life.

Request assistance from the light that surrounds you.

End your action by knowing it is done—that you are now in full control of your life.

Open your eyes.

If you were connected to an encephalograph that measures brain wave patterns, you would now find a change in your brain emissions. After the above action, your brain becomes more resonant with factors that are important for your survival and success.

These changes are very subtle, but experts can read them on the charts produced by this electronic biofeedback device.

Brain wave measurements can now be made at a distance. My alma mater, Massachusetts Institute of Technology, is doing the most advanced work in this field, but scientists from many universities are working on this.

Computers are being used to relate certain brain wave patterns to certain thoughts. In effect, this equipment will be able to read a person's thoughts a block away. The Pentagon has been reported to be backing the project financially. One of its agencies, The Advanced Research Projects Agency (ARPA) is reported to be handling the project which could be used in diplomatic matters and for defense. This raises some awesome possibilities of Big Brother monitoring our thoughts—all the more reason for you to become skilled at the use of psychotronic power to protect yourself, enhance your control over others and control your own destiny.

HOW TO STOP "JAMMING" YOUR OWN PSYCHOTRONIC SIGNALS

Would you like to be able to have a person come to you by merely beckoning with your finger? That person could be looking the other way, or, be even miles away, yet your psychotronic power will cause that inevitable result. The person will come.

All these years, you have not known this was possible. In fact, you have known it was impossible. This knowing must be altered. It acts as static to jam your mental attunement to your purpose.

The mind is the source of psychotronic power. All beliefs, expectations, and desires are like dials of the mind. A radio cannot be tuned to a station if every dial is not in its proper position.

The same is true of your mind. Every dial must be in its proper place

If you inject doubt or anxiety or fear it will not work, you are tuned into its not working.

"We have nothing to fear except fear itself," said Franklin D. Roosevelt in the early 1930's. He was talking about the fear of not having money or job in the depression. But fear attracts exactly what you do not want to happen.

Doubt attracts doubtful results.

Expectation and belief attracts what you expect and believe.

So, if you doubt, then you are not tuned in. Your doubt is quite effectively "jamming" your own psychotronic signals.

To build certainty in place of doubt, you must see your psychotronic signals being felt by another person. This means you must start with easy things first, and then move in to harder ones.

Easy projects are:

- Getting somebody to come around to your way of thinking overnight
- Getting a child to stop wetting his bed
- Getting a kind word from somebody who never said one to you before.

Harder projects are:

- Getting somebody to bring you a gift
- Getting somebody to move from here to there
- Getting somebody to offer their help to you.

We will cover the easy projects in this chapter. The harder types of control over others will be made easy in forthcoming chapters.

Start with these simple exercises:

1. Look at a person standing in front of you in an elevator, or waiting in line at a bank or theatre. Stare at the back of the neck, just under the hair line. The person will do something to prove to you that your "stare" energy was felt. He or she might move (uncomfortably), scratch his neck, or turn around and look at you.
2. Stare at your dog, cat, pet bird or somebody else's pet. Watch a dog's tail stop wagging and even droop, indicating fear. Watch the cat slink away. Watch for some nervous reaction in a bird.

3. When you are with a group of people have them play this ESP game. Somebody volunteers to leave the room. The rest agree on some object that the person who left must guess. As soon as the decision is made, you call the person back in. You hold the person's hand. Without actually looking in its direction, you and the others visualize the object while the person moves forward ahead of you toward where he feels pulled. Chances are he will move right to the object.

When you begin to get confirmation through one or more of these exercises, your belief and expectation will be functioning properly. You will not "jam" your own psychotronic signals. You will be able to exert these signals well focused and in sufficient strength to affect another person.

You are now ready to exercise control over people in moderate ways.

HOW TO GET OTHERS TO SEE THINGS YOUR WAY

Kay V. had a country farm with tenant farmers. A neighboring farmer and his wife were constantly making trouble for Kay's tenants—three young men.

One day a horse was found dead. The cause was not apparent. A week later a cow was found dead, again with no obvious cause of death. When a third animal (another horse) was found dead two weeks later, Kay suspected the neighboring farmer was poisoning her animals.

There was no way to prove it, but there was something she could do. She drew a rough sketch of a man and a woman. She put eyeglasses on the man just like the neighbor farmer wore. She wrote his name under the sketch. She did the same for his wife.

Holding the sketches in her hand she relaxed in a chair, closed her eyes and made believe she was speaking to her neighbors.

"If you are doing this, you are killing animals needlessly. I have never done you harm. Why should you do me harm? Do you know I can send hate energy to your crop and hurt its growth? But I would not do this. We need to live together in harmony and understanding. Your own hate is hurting you and your crops. How about it? Let's change from hate to harmony."

Occasionally, she would open her eyes and point at the sketch of the neighbor or his wife to emphasize a point.

She did this three or four times in as many days. The killings stopped. A few weeks later, the neighboring farmer lent her tenants one of his farm machines to help out with a project they were working on.

Here is the action plan for you to sway other persons to see things your way.

Action plan to sway a person to your side

Obtain a picture of that person or an article belonging to that person. If not obtainable, draw a simple sketch of a man, woman or child and label it with the name of the person, age, sex, and address. We will call this "the connection."

Sit in a chair with the connection in your hand. Close your eyes, relax and go to your special room by imagining you are there. Looking slightly upward, picture that person in your mind.

Present your case mentally to that person as if you were talking to a judge. Make your presentation logical, reasonable, convincing, but in thoughts not in words.

Appeal to that person's own selfish interest, showing how switching to your way will help that interest.

Use the connection from moment to moment by holding it up slightly above the horizontal, opening your eyes, looking at it steadfastly as if it were the person, and pointing at it with your fingers as if for emphasis.

End your psychotronic conversation with thoughts of friendship, understanding and loving rapport.

There is no voodoo or black magic in this action plan. It is working with psychotronic energy instead of sound energy. Sound energy is heard with the ears. Psychotronic energy is "heard" with the consciousness.

Since psychotronic energy is energy of consciousness, you need to use your consciousness, not your mouth, to communicate.

It is often a much more effective way.

RESONATE EVERY CELL OF YOUR BODY TO WORK YOUR WILL

Every cell in your body has consciousness. That consciousness is being affected moment to moment by your consciousness. Each cell has as its own goal: to do its job—be it a hair cell or a facial skin cell or a liver cell.

Each cell would do its job perfectly if it were not for the less-than-perfect aspects of our own consciousness.

Because we create a climate of fear, tension, anxiety or resentment, our hair cells are not healthy and the hair may fall out, or our facial complexion may be marred, or our liver may not be functioning at its best.

In the next chapter we will learn to improve the climate for perfect health with psychotronic power. Meanwhile, however, in order to permit your psychotronic power to work at its maximum at whatever level of health you are now, you need to contact the cells of your body and enlist their support.

At a recent ski competition, Jean-Claude Killy, winner of three Olympic gold medals, was unable to practice before the competition as he was recovering from an injury. Instead, he relaxed in his room and practiced mentally. He made believe he was skiing down the slope making every turn perfectly. It turned out to be one of his best races.

Another Olympic fencing contestant, Neil Glenesk, sits alone, eyes closed, visualizing his opponent and building up a feeling of hatred and aggression toward his opponent. This readies him psychologically for a rigorous fencing match.

Richard M. Suinn, a psychologist who works with American Olympic athletes, guides them in deep relaxation and high quality imagery in order for them to "feel" their muscles in action. An electro myograph shows muscles reacting as a relaxed skier imagines hitting the jumps in a downhill race.

Unconsciously you "talk" to your body cells constantly. A lack of confidence is communicated to them. Tension is. Fear is, too.

Have you felt a chill when you were afraid? Or, perhaps a crawling feeling on your skin, up and down your back, or feeling that your hair is rising on your head? A million years ago, when man was frightened by a possible enemy, he made himself look bigger by having his hair rise. It often helped him to survive. And so it was passed on from generation to generation in the survival of the fittest manner and still remains today as a vestige of caveman days.

You can communicate beneficially to your body cells just as easily as you can communicate harmfully. Your mind can be absorbed in worry and cause ulcers, pre-occupied with business pressures and cause heart disease. Your mind can also be absorbed in the peace of nature and rejuvenate your digestion system, be pre-occupied with tranquil pleasure and heal your heart.

The choice is yours.

Would you be willing to choose five minutes of "fence mending" and the restoration of friendly relations with your body cells right now?

All you need to do is to send your psychotronic energy to the cells, bearing the message of your appreciation and high regard. The result will be an enhancement of that psychotronic energy as the energy of the cells becomes aligned with yours.

You begin to resonate more harmoniously with your body cells. The result is better health and a stronger projection of psychotronic energy to work your will.

Action plan to have every cell in your body work for you

Find a position that is comfortable. In this action plan you can lie down, if you prefer.

Close your eyes and take a deep breath. As you exhale, feel like it's the end of a hard day and it feels so good to relax.

Be aware of your scalp. Feel the tingling of blood circulation there.

Picture your hair. See one hair enter your scalp.

Follow it down beneath the scalp. See it enlarged as a tree trunk in a forest of hair follicles.

Thank your hair for being your crowning glory.

Express gratitude now to your brain cells for being the computer of your body and the communications center.

Move your consciousness down. Thank your eyes, ears, taste buds, teeth for the excellent job they are doing.

Enter your throat and stomach. Praise the stomach cells for being such an efficient chemistry laboratory for the digestion of such a variety of foods.

Continue to express love, affection, and gratitude to your spleen, pancreas, liver, gall bladder, small intestines and on to your colon.

Say a kind word to your elimination system for a thankless, but essential job.

Get inside your bloodstream. Tell the white blood corpuscles to pass your love and thanks along to the others. Same with the red.

Stop off in your heart. Pay loving respect to this powerhouse. Then to your lungs for similar appreciation.

Finally back to your skull. Tell a bone cell to convey your gratitude to all bone cells. Tell a scalp cell to pass it on to all skin cells as you leave the way you entered.

Open your eyes feeling wide awake and better than you felt before.

This is a rather long action plan in words but if you read it through, once or twice you can get the idea of the physiological "itinerary." You do not have to sit with the book in your lap and open your eyes to see what to do next. Any way you travel through your body's systems, any way you express your respect, love and appreciation is the right way.

Your cells respond just as if the president of General Motors visited the production line to thank the workers. When the morale of your cells rises, you know it.

Everything appears improved–including your psychotronic power.

YOU HAVE THE POWER TO MELT CLOUDS

With your special place providing you with a link-up with the Cosmic Psychotronic Generator and with your body cells adding their power to yours, you have power that you do not believe you have.

That limited belief is still the major obstacle you have to contend with in moving from where you are in your life to new heights of power, health and success through psychotronic "miracles."

It is encumbent on me to show you easy ways to convince yourself that you have this power.

If you have gone through the action plans up to this point and have done some of the other tests and procedures suggested, you are ready to do what Ralph G. was able to do, what I am able to do, and what countless others have proven to themselves and their friends that they can do.

You can melt clouds.

Are you ready to upgrade your own confidence in your psychotronic power with a demonstration?

Ralph G. did not think he could do it. His life was a reflection of this negative approach. Failure after failure. It instructed him to select a wispy cloud above his head as the one he would melt and another wispy cloud to use as a "control." I explained that he would consider as positive proof the disappearance of the first wispy cloud without the full disappearance of the second wispy cloud.

He pointed to his object cloud and then to his "control" cloud. He relaxed, projected his consciousness to object cloud as if he was pointing a beam at it. Heat evaporates condensed water vapor. The cloud slowly disappeared. The "control" cloud changed, too, but it remained identifiable.

This had a profound effect on Ralph. For the first time he could see tangible evidence of the power of his thought energy. This tangible evidence was happening in his life right along, but he was not putting two and two together. Now he could see how the energy of his consciousness was a very real power shaping his life. From then on he used it positively and his life reflected this new polarity—success after success.

You will be able to perform this cloud-melting demonstration to your own satisfaction, too. Here is how:

Action plan to melt a cloud

Select an object cloud (wispy) and an equivalent "control" cloud.

Relax in a standing position (do not sit or lie).

Stare at the object cloud. Ignore the control cloud.

Imagine that you are sending a beam of conscious energy to that cloud.

Reach your hands upward and point the first three fingers of each hand at the object cloud knowing that this increases the psychotronic power penetrating it.

Expect it to react by melting away.

Compare the change to the "control" cloud.

You can probably do this the first day. If the results are not convincing, practice the action plans that precede this and try again.

It is not important that you melt a cloud, but it is important that you know and accept your psychotronic power.

When you do melt a cloud, let it go at that. To continue to do so, whether for fun or vanity, is a waste of power.

You are better off using the power to improve your life.

A WAY TO UPGRADE YOUR LIFE AND TAKE THESE PERSONS IMPORTANT TO YOU ALONG WITH YOU

Now that you know the immensity of your psychotronic power, you need to plan on how to use it in your life.

The first step is to set priorities, what you want most—an executive position? More friends? Better health? A trip? New home or car?

Put everything you want on separate cards. Break each goal down into its components.

For instance, make out health cards by first making out a card for that aspect of your health that needs immediate improvement. Then separate cards for other health problems right down to halting coughs or colds or other health nuisances.

Do the same for possessions. Whatever you want deserves a separate card.

Do the same for others in your family—separate cards for separate goals.

When you have ten or twenty file cards filled out, number them in order of importance. Then place number one in front of the others, number two behind it, etc.

You are now ready to perform an action plan that will trigger every one of these goals to realization.

Action plan to upgrade your life

Go to your "special room" and relax in the special chair with the cards in your hand.

Hold the cards with the tips of your fingers, top priority on top.

Gaze at the top card. See a mental picture of it coming true. If it involves a goal, see yourself having already received that goal.

Spend about as many seconds on this first card as you have cards.

Place the card in back of the rest and proceed to gaze at the card next in line in the same way, but a second less.

Go through the whole set of cards in this way, spending less and less on each.

Repeat the procedure for the first card only when you reach it.

Leave your special room mentally, knowing action has been triggered to upgrade your life according to your cards.

Save the cards for future repetition of this daily, eliminating cards as goals are reached.

Congratulations! You are on your way.

4

BETTER HEALTH AT THE SNAP OF YOUR FINGERS WITH PSYCHOTRONIC ENERGY

In this chapter you learn to stop pain in yourself and in others. You become a psychic healer. You are able to use your hands and eyes to help correct your own physical problems and help others without even being near them. You are able to harness psychotronic energy to help keep yourself and others in good health.

Have you heard of palming? It is recommended for tense, tired executives. You place your palms over your eyes, base of palms resting on your cheek bones. Hold this position for two minutes while you picture yourself away from your desk at some more tranquil location.

What is really happening through palming? Of course, every

time you close your eyes and take your mind off your tensions you are giving yourself a moment of restful rejuvenation. But placing the hands over the eyes adds another element to this.

That element is psychotronic energy.

Your life energy radiated through your fingers and recycled through your eyes, is built up. You feel the difference in seconds.

You can place your hands on another person and get confirmation of this effect. The late Ambrose Worrell, working with his wife, Olga, created a clinic for healing through the "laying on of hands." They were a dramatic example of the power of psychotronic energy to heal. Their hands focused psychotronic energy into the ailing, and effected changes for the better in moments.

Olga Worrell has since made herself available to numerous scientists interested in the study of psychotronic energy. One experiment in which she held an enzyme in her hand for a few minutes, showed that enzyme to be at a greater level of activity than a control batch which she did not hold. Also, a batch of enzymes damaged under the ultra-violet light was shown to be restored when held in her hands.

Similarly, water when held in her hands and sent with control samples to three separate spectroscopic laboratories, exhibited similar shifts in the three analyses, indicating that human psychotronic energy might be making molecular changes in matter such as water.

HOW TO USE YOUR HANDS TO STOP PAIN IN YOUR BODY IN MINUTES

Your hands are a channel for psychotronic energy. You can help heal another person. Try it. The next time somebody has a pain in his stomach or back or head. Hold your hands on the affected area. Do not massage, or rub or manipulate—unless you have a medical license.

The laying on of hands is a spiritual process. You become a channel for spiritual healing. In more scientific terms this means that your psychotronic energy is being added to the person's own psychotronic energy.

In Japan there is a healing practice known as Reiki. It is the laying on of hands. It is taught only to a select few who are usually not permitted to teach it to others. However, a Honolulu woman who was healed by it received permission and has been teaching it throughout the United States. A Honolulu doctor became interested and asked for a treatment. It was so effective, he has seen to it that this woman be given hospital privileges whenever asked to help hospitalized patients.

Dr. Edward Mitchell, in association with other researchers, has investigated the laying on of hands and found energy at work in measurable ways. His work and that of other psychotronic scientists is moving toward more understanding of the practical ways to apply uses of this energy for specific health problems.

Meanwhile, pain remains the most insidious of illness symptoms. Drugs are not the perfect answer. While they bring relief, they cause other problems.

You can use your conscious energy to end pain. It is done by focusing it through your hands. Psychotronic energy, so focused, can actually numb the nerves. Pain then ceases.

The next Action Plan tells you how you can do this using your visualizing power. You need not "go" to your special room. You can imagine it all happening where you are. It involves an imaginary bucket of ice water.

A word of warning: pain is nature's way of saying there is a problem. Use this method only for first aid, or temporary relief. If pain returns, see your doctor.

Action plan to relieve pain

Relax where you are. Close your eyes.

Deepen your relaxation.

Pretend there is a bucket of ice water by the side of your chair.

Place your hand in the bucket by letting it hang down at the side of your chair.

Feel the icy cold water, the cracked ice or cubes.

Remember when you had your hand in ice cold water before. Recall how it feels.

Make your hand feel as numb as it did then.

Keep your hand in the bucket of ice water until it gets more numb. This might take two or three minutes.

Take your hand out of the water, and test it for numbness by pinching. Pinch your other hand to compare. Return it to the ice water if necessary.

Touch the pained area of your body with the numb hand.

Instruct the numbness to move out of your hand to the pained area, then . . .

Rub your hand and instruct it to return to normalcy.

End your session, feeling better than you did before—the pain relieved.

Tom B. was hit by a car while riding a motorcycle. He fell free of the vehicle but mangled his foot and knee in the process. Instantly, he touched these areas to relieve the pain. He was then able to rest comfortably until medical help arrived.

Once you perform the Action Plan described above, you are able to merely "think" that your hand is in ice water and it will respond. That response becomes faster and faster the more you practice. Ultimately, you make your hand numb at will.

Joan C. was one of three persons with a very low level of pain tolerance and she fainted at the sight of blood. She studied psychotronics and especially the numbing technique.

One day Joan was cutting the lawn. The mower jammed. She attempted to free what was stuck in the cutter. She succeeded but did not withdraw her hand fast enough. She suffered a deep cut. She saw the blood start to spurt.

Instantly she thought, "Hand well. No panic. No pain. No bleeding."

She went into the house to wash her hand. Her husband took one look at the cut and said, "We're taking you to the hospital. That needs stitches." By now the bleeding had stopped, and there was no pain, but Joan agreed to go just to satisfy her husband. At the hospital, no stitches were needed. Healing had already started. Only a bandage was applied. When the bandage was removed a few days later there was not even a scar.

You can use a simple biofeedback device to speed your progress. Before you hold your hand in the imaginary bucket of ice water, hold the bulb of a thermometer in your fingers for a couple of minutes until it registers your finger temperature. Then insert your hand in the imaginary ice water and check the thermometer every few minutes. When you see the most dramatic drop—three degrees is entirely possible—you know that the way you just imaged is the best and most effective way.

UNDERSTANDING THE POWER OF YOUR HANDS TO HEAL

Your hands are powerful, precise servants of your mind.

Man's imaging faculty begins the creative process.

Then his hands take over.

Your hands have some 25 joints and over fifty different possible motions.

Your hands have the ability to create or destroy material comforts, to create a new culture or destroy an old one.

You reinforce your physical balance with your hands, you emphasize your speech and communication with your hands, and you focus your psychotronic energy with your hands.

People understand the first two, but not the last.

Sometimes, the mind and the hands working together to do evil, shake people up to understand this power better.

- A Haitian witchdoctor creates a doll in the image of a person. He puts pins in that doll. The person becomes deathly ill.
- A soccer team in Kenya, Africa, asks a local witchdoctor for help in defeating a rival visiting team. The witchdoctor takes a cat as symbol of the rival team. He strangles the cat. The home team wins.
- An Indian fakir drops human excrement in front of an enemy's house. He makes some passes with his hands. The enemy is taken ill.

You do not need to see evil done to understand the psychotronic power of your hands. The following scene takes place regularly in the author's home, but it is also happening in scores of other places throughout the United States.

A dozen people are seated comfortably. Their eyes are closed. They are at their relaxed alpha level of mind and have gone into their "special room."

"Mr. Roy Jones, 43, of Memphis, Tennessee has been told he has a kidney stone. Please detect the problem and make corrections." The host reads this from a list.

Hands begin to move. One person appears to be moving an

imaginary man higher and higher so he can observe all of the anatomy in close detail. Another person is turning the body around. Now someone snaps his fingers to make an area brighter for his easier "examination."

A few people start grinding an imaginary stone between their fingers, pulverizing it. Other hand motions occur suggestive of cutting, removing, sewing.

After a few minutes, the host reads another problem case from his list and hands begin to move once more.

The next time these groups meet, they hear about recoveries, improvements, and healings. "Mr. Jones passed the stone the next morning."

Your hands have healing powers. These powers are naturally there. However, your lack of awareness that you have these powers in your hands acts to diminish and throttle the powers.

Increase your awareness of your hands' powers and you permit those powers to be restored.

This is already happening. It happened as you began to read this chapter. Kirlian photographs of your hands when you started, and now, would reflect a difference.

Evergy is increasing in your hands. You can accelerate this increase with the next Action Plan.

Action plan for increasing your hands' healing power

Relax deeply. Eyes closed. Deep breaths.

Go to your special room and sit under the skylight.

Imagine light entering the skylight, flowing through your hands.

Hold your hands up and open your eyes.

"See" light pouring out of your hands. "See" your hands radiant with healing light.

End your session, knowing your hands are even more powerful than before.

HOW PSYCHOTRONIC HEALING TAKES PLACE

The healing work undertaken by the people who moved their hands as described earlier in this chapter is conducted under a number of training disciplines today. The author is a trainer in one of these disciplines—Silva Mind Control—from which a number of offshoots have come about.

The training consists of accepting mental conditioning that you can do it, and of setting up a methodology to proceed.

The fact that acceptance produces the results is not new to science. We are no better than we think we are. This has been the message of psychiatrists and psychologists through the past decades. Self-image seems to be the only limiting factor to human behavior.

The methodology of working at a subjective or imaginary level is based on the same procedures used at an objective or material level. We work with our hands at more physical work. Working with these same hands, even though it is imaginary work, adds energy to that work—psychotronic energy.

This is called psychic healing. It appears to be an energy process that is channeled by the thoughts of the picturing person into the affected parts of the ill person.

This energy transfer is the key to healing, but it does not actually do the healing. What does the healing is the same healing process that is always at work naturally. Only now, reinforced by outside energy, it is able to make faster progress.

There is another factor involved here that is important. Each person has the choice to come or go. That means be alive or not be alive. Many cases of illness are subconscious death wishes beginning to be manifest.

A psychic healer visualizes a sick person healed. The healing takes place.

The same psychic healer visualizes another person well who has that same sickness. This time a healing does not take place. Why?

Chances are that the second person subconsciously rejected the psychotronic energy sent for healing.

Healing by prayer, whether the prayerful ones fully realize this or not, assists an ill person in two ways:

1. An argument in favor of life is presented at a superconscious level.
2. Psychotronic healing energy is supplied.

In other words, the plea for assistance directed to a Higher Level, produces a change in the ill person's subconscious death wish, or wish to be ill.

It is as if a silent discussion takes place something like this.

Superconscious: "Your work is not done. Get well."
Ill person's subconscious: "I am not worthy, not capable, not wanted here. I deserve to be punished for failing."
Superconscious: "You are worthy and wanted. You deserve to be rewarded with good health and happy life experiences. Here is healing energy. Accept it."
Ill person's subconscious: "All right, I accept it."

Bill G., 42, was not improving from growing depression that took his appetite away and was leaving him progressively weaker. His case was placed before a group of psychic healers without any results.

Then an exorcist handled the case, could find no evidence of possession, but had "a talk" with Bill's soul. The imaged conversation purported to show Bill unwilling to live because of a spouse's infidelity. The exorcist counseled Bill in his imagination. Counseling at this level produced a very real change of heart. In other words, the change at the soul level, or inner level, produced an immediate change at the physical or outer level. Bill's appetite, and mood, improved steadily from that day on. He became more understanding of his wife's needs and actions. Their marriage improved.

Acceptance of psychotronic healing is necessary if it is to work.

HOW PRAYER FITS IN WITH PSYCHOTRONIC HEALING

Prayer is acceptance of healing.

In effect, it is saying: I got myself in here, now I want to get out. Help me.

So often faith healers of great renown, die of some disease. People become disillusioned. Why couldn't they heal themselves?

The answer is as simple as one and one make two. If you are ill, and somebody adds his psychotronic energy to yours, a significant outpouring of that energy is added. But even if you have techniques for increasing your own psychotronic energy, it has already been lessened by your own illness and the increase, though it may double it, may still leave it less than normal.

That is why healers go to other healers.

It is easy to lift another person up, but impossible to lift yourself up.

When you pray for healing, you are doing the equivalent of going to "another healer." The appeal for help constitutes both the switching on of additional psychotronic power and acceptance of that power.

Where does it come from? The Universal Psychotronic Generator. You might call this the Generator Of Divinity (GOD), if you will.

Healing was once one of the main functions of the church. After centuries of it having been played down, it is now returning in many denominations.

The healing Christ light within us, the healing gift of God, or the healing spirit of the Holy Ghost are some of the religious terms once in use that are now returning.

There is no difference in the process as the words differ. And there is no difference in the process as approached by the church or by science despite the different words used.

The similarity between the methods of faith healers and the methods of psychotronic healers becomes apparent when washed clean of word differences.

Both require a strong desire to effect a cure.

Both require an expectation and belief that a cure will be effected.

Both require a total absorption of the mind in the process. Some call this concentration; but this word denotes effort. Rather it is a relaxed involvement in the project.

Both require a picture of the problem in the mind of the healer and then a picture of the salvation.

There are some exceptions to the latter. Christian Science, for instance, sees only the perfection, not the problem.

The more people you have working for you, the more the energy.

Prayer groups are successful. So are psychic groups.

You can help yourself in many ways. And we will now deal with some of these ways. But don't sell prayer short, or prayer groups.

And, remember, in serious illness your psychotronic energy needs the reinforcement of others.

Polish medical doctors have reported how they are studying psychotronic energy at work in the medical profession. They see some medicines working for some doctors but not for others, treating the same illnesses. They also see how when a doctor is treating one patient for whom he has a great rapport, his ability to be effective for other patients is greatly diminished.

Both facts point to something going on in the doctor-patient relationship that is closely associated with matters beyond the pills, shots, and therapy—with the energy of their consciousness.

HOW TO FREE YOURSELF OF CERTAIN PHYSICAL CONDITIONS

A woman who studied with me told me her daughter was despondent over her poor complexion. "She is too embarrassed to come to you for help. Is there anything I can do for her? she asked.

"What is your daughter's name?" I inquired.

"Betty."

I took a piece of paper and wrote:

"Dear Betty,

1. Take a large photo of yourself, just head and shoulders.
2. Carry it with you for three days, put it under your pillow for three nights.
3. Take typewriter correction fluid and white over your facial skin.
4. Post the photo up on your bedroom door where you can see it as you come and go. Stare at it."

Betty's mother saw me in three weeks. "She followed your instructions," she exclaimed with great surprise, as it was the first time Betty did what she was told. "She's 75% better and now a hit with boys who have known her all along. She said to give you this." I opened the large envelope. It was Betty's picture. On the whited face she had typed the word "Thanx."

If you do the Action Plan to increase the psychotronic power in your hands, as provided earlier in this chapter, you are able to help yourself in many ways.

Action plan to relieve physical problems

Relax easily, closing your eyes, taking a deep breath and feeling an improvement has already begun.

See yourself with the problem. Review it.

Change to a picture of the solution. See yourself perfect. See yourself relieved of the condition.

Point the fingers of your hand at the affected area.

Snap your fingers, saying "Gone!"

I myself had a problem with my eyes. They would be very dry at night, so dry that I would awake with one eye sticking to the socket and causing pain when coming loose. Then it would tear profusely. Eye doctors gave me salves and drops but none helped.

After years of accepting this problem, I decided I now had the knowledge to get rid of it. In doing the above action plan, I used a command in conjunction with the picture of the solution: "My eyes will be properly lubricated until I awake."

After years of wrestling with this problem, it disappeared with just one session and has never returned.

YOUR PSYCHOTRONIC ENERGY CAN HEAL OTHERS

Bringing your own psychotronic energy to bear on your own physical problem is fine but two people are better than one.

Another person can help you to heal yourself better than you can heal yourself alone.

Maybe that is what is behind Jesus' statement "where any two shall gather in my name."

Here is how to go about helping another person to heal. This is on a spiritual level. It is the use of psychotronic power. It is never done in the presence of that person. This is to avoid any misunderstanding that the medical authorities might get.

Psychotronic healing is legal, just as prayer healing is legal. Both are the exercise of the energy of consciousness–on a nonmaterial level. Nonmaterial is spiritual. You are therefore protected by the freedom of religion guarantee of our Constitution.

Spiritual healing should not be undertaken as a substitute for medical attention. Rather, it should be utilized as first aid before medical attention can arrive, and be continued as an adjunct to that attention.

Here is the basic Action Plan for healing others.

Action plan for healing another person

Relax and go to your special "room."

Invite the ill person in your imagination to enter the room.

"See" the person standing in front of you, complaining of the problem.

Fix the person with your hands. See explanation below.

Let the final image of this person be one of total fitness.

End your session, knowing the person is being restored to total health.

A word about using your hands. This adds to the reality of this psychotronic work. The imagination has been so brainwashed into thinking it is just fantasy that it needs help in making the procedure as real as scientists now recognize the imagination to be.

Also, the hands help to focus psychotronic energy where needed.

Energy we call electricity is the energy of free electrons. It follows the patterns of these electrons. The more free electrons in a substance, the better it conducts electrical energy.

Heat energy is the energy of molecular motion. It needs contact to pass its heat from a hot object to a cold one.

Psychotronic energy is the energy of consciousness. It does not follow the patterns of electrical, heat, light, or any other energy. It goes where thought goes. And that is not very limiting.

Seeing a person free of a disease sends psychotronic energy to that person no matter where; and that energy performs work toward healing.

When you point your fingers at your imaged picture of a person you increase the flow of your healing psychotronic energy.

The hands are tools of the consciousness.

A truck has dented the fender of a taxi. Both drivers are in the street shouting at each other. Their hands are flying as they talk, gesticulating to add emphasis (energy) to their mental (conscious) conviction.

A child has disobeyed. The mother warns the child that the next time will bring a spanking. She points at the child to "get her point across." She shakes her finger to make the threat more emphatic.

You can use your hands in the healing process to emphasize your point. Anything you do with your hands is helpful:

- Point at the imagined person
- Rub on an imaginary salve
- Spray with an imaginary disease dissolver
- Snap your fingers to "command" healing
- Erase a blemish, or lung spots

- Pulverize a stone
- Sew up a wound.

The hands help your consciousness effectuate the relief, improvement, or cure.

YOU HELP YOUR OWN HEALTH WHEN YOU HELP OTHERS

The author was asked by a woman with a bone spur to assist her to remove it. It was getting increasingly irritated by her clothing, being located at the back of her shoulder.

"I'm going to have it removed by surgery," she explained, "but I thought maybe you could make this unnecessary."

"When are you planning to have the operation?" I asked.

"I enter the hospital tomorrow," she replied.

Well, that was not much time to create a physical change in something as rigid as a bone spur, but I could not ignore the request.

That night I relaxed, imaged the woman, and went through the motions with my hands of sawing off the spur.

She went ahead with the operation on schedule and the matter was forgotten. But about a week later, I noticed something strange about my left elbow. It was always very pointed and pronounced. Now it was rounded, just like my right elbow.

I had removed a spur all right—not hers, but my own.

Whenever you help other people, you help yourself. It is as if your psychotronic energy is "repaid" by that person's psychotronic energy.

Every time you go to your relaxed "alpha" level of mind, whether to help others or yourself, your body and mind receive instant benefits.

Individuals involved in the use of psychotronic power, or in such relaxation practices as yoga, self-hypnosis, or meditation report improved memory, concentration and creativity. Many claim improvements in their personality, self-confidence and job leadership. Many also report the correction of unwanted habits such as excessive eating, drinking and smoking.

Most common improvements claimed for the relaxed state, regularly attained, are better sleeping habits, less tension and nervousness, fewer colds and headaches, and greater control over their personal relationships.

You have the greatest power on earth in your consciousness. Just tuning in this power by relaxing and imagining brings dramatic personal improvements.

Focusing this power on a specific problem brings "miraculous" results.

HOW YOU CAN "SEE" HEALTH PROBLEMS IN OTHERS

A medical conference was held in Tucson, Arizona in 1975 to share research and experiences on new directions in medicine, especially the way the mind and body can work together in the healing process.

This National Congress on Integrative Health heard Dr. V. Norman Shealy, a surgeon at the University of Wisconsin, report on an 18-month study of how people with so-called psychic ability can make medical diagnosis, without the radiation and other medical risks, just as accurately as physicians can with the aid of modern equipment.

Dr. Shealy's report told of how clairvoyants were given a sketch of the human body and then given the name and address of a patient. The clairvoyants would then indicate on the sketch where the problem area was and tell something about it. They were over 75% accurate and in some cases corrected faulty medical diagnosis.

Besides clairvoyants, the research also used numerologists, palmists and astrologists, most of whom had never seen the patients but who were given the necessary photos, birthdates, palm prints and other similar information required by their unorthodox approach.

Dr. Shealy pointed to the advantage of using psychics for the hundreds of thousands of expensive and possibly risky X-ray dye-tracer tests done yearly. The X-ray tests are 80% accurate with a one percent risk of causing a problem, he noted, while the psychics could be 98 percent accurate with no risks.

If you wish to help another person who has a problem not responding to medical care, this might require you to determine the nature of the problem. It might be quite different than the medical treatment assumes, or it might include other undiagnosed factors.

You can determine this through your psychotronic energy. It is not called diagnosis. Only duly licensed health practitioners may diagnose. It is called psychotronic discernment. It differs from diagnosis in two ways:

1. It is done at a distance, never in the subject's presence.
2. The subject is not told of the problem discerned.

All you need for successful psychotronic discernment is:

- The ability to relax
- A visual imagination
- A desire to help the person
- The expectation and belief that you can succeed.

A number of commercial courses give training in this ability. One student who graduated Silva Mind Control attended a follow-up workshop and complained to the instructor. "I can't do it."

"Stand up, John!" ordered the teacher. "I have a card in here in my shirt pocket. On it is the name and address of a person with physical problems. I am going to walk down the aisle toward you; by the time I reach you I want you to tell me what is wrong with this person."

He started to walk toward John. John acted flustered for a moment. Closed his eyes then blurted out, "She has an amputated right arm and spots on her lungs."

The instructor pulled out the card and showed it to John. He was exactly right!

Graduates of this course call psychotronic discernment "detection," and psychotronic healing "correction." Untold thousands of cases of accurate detection and effective correction have been experienced by the now hundreds of thousands of graduates of this training. This year, its founder Jose Silva announced the availability of this training free to ministers of all faiths, in an effort to return faith healing to the church.

If you feel you have the four requirements for successful psychotronic discernment spelled out above, then you are ready to perform this Action Plan.

Action plan for psychotronic discernment of illness

Relax in your special room under the skylight.

Invite the ill person to enter and stand before you.

Scan his body up and down being aware of any part that your attention is attracted to.

Point at that part of the body and request that it become transparent.

Snap the fingers to make the affected part bigger and brighter for easier viewing.

Discern the problem, by asking the affected part what the abnormality is.

Accept the answer that comes to mind.

Fix the person with your hands using any imagined tool or medicine that comes to mind.

"See" the person perfect.

End your relaxation, knowing the situation is changed.

Many doctors are now giving new credence to the importance of thoughts and feelings in the healing picture. Consciousness makes us ill. Consciousness can make us well.

The use of positive visualization by the patient is slowly entering the physician's repertoire.

Perhaps the physician's own positive visualization for his patients will come next. Then the miracle of psychotronic power will be brought fully to bear on the problems of human health.

HAND SIGNALS THAT WORK HEALTH MIRACLES FOR YOU

There is no reason to list the kinds of physical problems that respond to your use of positive imaging. They all respond.

The cause-effect relation still exists and some conditions are being caused as fast as they are being corrected.

Shirley B. got rid of the symptoms of her cold in twelve hours.

Percy L. got rid of a persistent low backache in minutes, and it did not return.

Isaac T. got rid of a painful swelling in his sprained ankle in one hour.

If you have pains, aches, swelling or other discomfort which you wish to relieve, here is an Action Plan that can bring results in a matter of minutes. If the condition persists, see your doctor, but for immediate, "first aid" for yourself or another person, use this Action Plan:

First aid action plan to obtain relief from a painful condition

Relax wherever you are.

Point to the area affected by the condition, indicating its boundaries.

Shape with your hands the kind of container that would be needed if this condition could fit a container.

Describe the color of this painful condition, as if it had a color.

Do the same for its taste and smell, if it had a taste and smell.

Again point to the area affected indicating its changed boundaries.

Again shape with your hands the reduced size of the container now needed.

Repeat, if necessary. If then not fully disappeared . . .

Place the condition in an imaginary red balloon.

Tap the balloon with your hand, sending it away.

The dramatic improvements affected by this method demonstrate the power of psychotronic energy in this field of work.

Bertha M. had chronic backache. When the author offered at a group meeting to demonstrate this ability of thought to get rid of pain, she hastened to volunteer.

She pointed to the lower back. The pain would fit a large bowl. It was dark gray in color, she said, tasted bitter and smelled moldy. We went through the routine together again. This time the pain would fit a cup. It was light gray, had hardly any taste and the smell was musty. When I asked her to locate the pain again, it was gone.

She returned to the meeting a month later and reported that her ten-year-old pain had never returned.

Pain is subjective. When you use the energy of consciousness to make pain objective—so much like an object that it has shape, color, smell and taste—it is no longer pain.

You may tell another person how to do this. You may even lead him through the line of questioning. But, be sure not to touch, diagnose, or instruct in any way. Just ask. And let the person's own psychotronic energy work his own miracle.

5

HOW TO USE YOUR EYES TO FOCUS YOUR PSYCHOTRONIC ENERGY ON BULLIES, TYRANTS, PESKY NEIGHBORS, AND OTHER OBNOXIOUS PEOPLE YOU WANT TO CONTROL

You learn how to control people who are getting in the way of your job, your love life, or your happiness. You use a magic weapon and they will never know what hit them. You also learn how to create an impregnable shield that protects you from psychic or mental attack by others. Can a simple act like drinking coffee be used to harness psychotronic energy? Learn how to make such acts trigger changes in people—the changes you want. Learn, too, how to use geometric shapes and basic colors to get what you want faster.

This is a competitive world.

People take advantage of other people.

Slavery may be ended, but some people still enslave other people in different ways. There is economic slavery, emotional slavery, sexual slavery, political slavery, and many other avenues of human exploitation.

These are all power plays. Individuals seek more and more control over more and more people. It happens in business, government, society and family life.

When you are exposed to this power, you feel it in a variety of ways.

- A supervisor can be unreasonable
- A suitor can be overly aggressive
- A neighbor can be irritating
- A law enforcement official can be mean
- A religious leader can be intrusive
- An acquaintance can bully or gossip
- An employer can threaten

If you are faced with any obnoxious use of personal power, you have the power to combat it—your psychotronic power.

Psychotronic power works at an unconscious level. Your enemies won't ever know what "hit" them.

YOUR EYES CAN FOCUS PSYCHOTRONIC POWER IN FORCEFUL WAYS

For centuries legends about the "evil eye" have persisted. Rasputin, the Russian monk whose healing powers made him influential in Czarist circles, was said to have the power to command through his eyes.

Hypnotists today still use eye contact to gain cooperation from their subjects. The hypnotic eye has become a symbol of power in many cultures.

Besides being the center of sight and therefore the natural visual center of person-to-person contact, the eye is a powerful transmitter of psychotronic energy.

Just as fingers focus psychotronic energy, millions of tiny optic cells both receive light energy and transmit psychotronic energy.

There are two secrets which can take the power away from tyrants and bullies who try to push you around and place that power in you:

> *Secret No. 1:* Holding a person in the stare of your eyes makes you the sender, then the receiver.
>
> *Secret No. 2:* Whatever you send them, you receive back.

Most people who throw their weight around, get buried or "snowed" in the end. People who hate are in turn hated. People who are obnoxious in any way to others, reap an obnoxious reward themselves.

What we put out, we get back. It is called the law of attraction in the West, the law of karma in the East. There is no place you can go to escape it. It is a law that operates like the law of gravity.

Knowing these two secrets, you are able to turn the tables on any enemy. But you cannot turn the tables on an enemy by holding him in eye contact and sending animosity. You are only feeding the fires of his own doing.

You cannot send pesky thoughts to a pesky person. You only help that person to become more pesky, especially toward you.

You cannot send hate to a hateful person and expect a change. You are reinforcing the unwanted condition.

The way to change animosity, peskiness, and hate is to send their opposites.

The miracle of psychotronic energy used to subdue bullies and tyrants is that you do not become the victor in the sense that you can bully the bully, but rather the whole situation becomes subdued.

HOW TO TRANSFORM PESKY PEOPLE WITH PSYCHOTRONIC POWER

Why not change a pesky situation right now? Why not use your psychotronic power focused through your eyes to change polarity from hostility to harmony?

You will need a picture or sketch of the person which will be used as the "connection" similar to the Action Plan to sway a person to your side described in Chapter 3.

Draw a simple sketch and label it with the name, age, sex and address of the pesky person or bully you wish to straighten out. You are then ready to begin.

The first step, as you will see in the Action Plan following, is to see the picture as the person rather than a diagram or photo. Spend some time before you begin creating this illusion. See the person as being *in* the picture or sketch.

Action plan to subdue a tyrant or bully:

Gaze at the picture keeping your eyes open as you relax and imagine yourself to be in your "special room" under the skylight.

Understand the picture as being the person.

See the person not as a bully but as a person tormented by some personal problem.

Feel sympathy and understanding for the person.

Let the understanding shift gradually to a feeling of warmth and respect, even love.

End this session feeling as if it has been a real encounter.

Repeat several times a day until a complete transformation has taken place in the person.

PICTURES, STRANDS OF HAIR, NAIL CUTTINGS, CLOTHING–WHY THEY ACT AS CONNECTIONS TO A REAL PERSON

Moslems and Hindus have practices that utilize psychotronic energy without, of course, knowing exactly what physical laws are at work. It is called magic. More often than not it is black magic–used for doing in an adversary–rather than white magic–helping some person out of a difficulty.

Sometimes black is combined with white. For instance, the excrement of a sick person may be wrapped in an attractive package tied with the person's hair. Usually the package is left on the highway for the curious to open. When this happens, the curious person is likely to catch the disease. This is intended to take the disease away from the sick person and accelerate a cure.

Frequently the package is placed in the home of an enemy. This black magic has its risks, because if the enemy has knowledge of black magic, too, he gets a red hot poker and jabs it into the package of excrement, knowing that at that very moment, the person to whom it belongs will feel a sharp hot pain in his anus.

You do not need a picture to reach and change another person, much less a package of excrement. But these "connections" have been used quite successfully as a means of directing the energy of consciousness to find its target.

The energy of consciousness needs no such help. It is directed at the person by your knowing the person to whom you want to send that energy.

Colors heal people of certain problems. Color therapy has been used quite successfully. Now it is known that the photograph of the person placed under the healing light is just as effective.

In the Southwest a firm that was engaged in cropdusting discovered that aerial photographs treated with the spray had the same effects as if the entire fields were sprayed. The insects responded.

A picture of a person identifies that person in the universal mind. So does a strand of hair, nail cutting, or piece of clothing.

Stephen was despondent. His fiancée had broken off their relationship and he felt like ending his life. There was nothing left for him.

I convinced him there was plenty left for him. Even a chance to win back his fiancée. I gave him psychotronic instructions.

Stephen held a blouse left behind by his girl friend when she left him for another man. He used it in place of a picture in the Chapter 3 Action Plan. Within a few weeks she traveled over a thousand miles to return to him.

He did not have to use that article. The universal mind could contact his girl friend merely by the desire of his own mind. The conductor of psychotronic energy takes that energy instantly to where consciousness wants it to go.

Your consciousness, your mind, is in contact with universal mind. Your desire to contact a person defines that person as the recipient of your psychotronic energy. There are no mistakes, no wrong numbers.

There can be a dozen people of that same name, even age and sex, in that town but your knowing whom you wish to contact makes it happen, faultlessly.

The only help the "connection" provides, be it picture or hair strand, is that your closeness to the person is enhanced.

We are fooled by distance. Distance says to us in effect, "Out of reach."

The "connection" being in our hand, helps to overcome the conditioning of the environment which makes distance an obstacle.

If we think we cannot contact that person, we cannot. This is fortunate, indeed, for: if we think we can, we can.

New thought religions are recognizing a universal mind. Unity and Religious Science are examples. Ernest Holmes, founder of the latter, saw universal mind, which he capitalized, as individualized in each person. He explained it as an "infinite knowingness." Just as a light bulb utilizes electrical energy and lights up a limited space, he said, so each person uses some portion of the universal mind in a limited way but without making it any less universal.

We can use more of universal mind or less. The choice is ours.

If you created a special room by the Action Plan in a previous chapter you made the choice. You hooked into the Cosmic Psychotronic Generator, which produces the energy of consciousness of the universal mind.

Uri Geller, whose bending of forks and fixing of watches with psychotronic energy has made him famous, cannot always do it. He seems to get "the nod" from something outside of himself. It is as if universal mind also has the choice to use our mind or not.

Since the universal mind is not divided against itself, it cannot oppose itself. It is creative. It created the universe. So it is aligned with constructive, creative purposes—the solving of human problems, human growth and maturity, health and happiness.

Tyrants? You have universal mind working for you. Look at history. The road is marked with the gravestones of tyrants.

HOW TO HASTEN A TYRANT'S DEMISE

Tyrants come in all sizes. There are landlord tyrants who tyrannize tenants, and tenant tyrants who tyrannize landlords and landlord's property.

There are employers that make life miserable for employees, and employees that make life just as miserable for employers.

Husbands tyrannize wives and vice versa.

A young man who worked for a large department store was questioned by the security guards regarding some inventory shortages. He was so incensed that he told his wife that he was going to put a strong laxative in the guards' food at the forthcoming company picnic. Days before the picnic, he was again questioned. This time the security team had evidence which came so close to incriminating him in a crime of which he was innocent that for two days he had a severe case of diarrhea.

He got back what he put out.

What do you put out to a tyrant that will end his career but which does not return harm to you? The answer is *love.*

"Preposterous!" you say. "How can you love a tyrant?"

Ask animal trainer Boone who made a Hollywood star out of Strongheart in the silent film days. When Boone was given Strongheart to train, the dog was hostile and uncooperative. Each day was worse than the day before. The dog became a threat to Boone's reputation. He felt tyrannized by the dog. And no doubt the feeling was mutual.

One late afternoon following a tempestuous time with the dog, Boone was resting on a grassy knoll watching the sunset when he noticed the dog was also watching the sunset. He looked at the dog. The dog looked at him.

From that special moment on, everything changed. The dog was no longer a tyrant to Boone, and Boone felt more inclination to work in a genial way with the dog. Success followed.

What also followed was Boone's adventures with wild horses that he was able to ride by feeling a oneness with them; rattlesnakes that refused to strike when Boone felt love for them; and even a housefly that behaved when Boone felt respect for it.

How can you love a tyrant? Feel a kinship that life brings.

You can take it in easy stages. In the Action Plan that follows, you are asked to imagine yourself with the tyrant in "a scene." Start doing the Action Plan with a scene you can tolerate.

Charles B. had a problem with his neighbor. The neighbor accused him of permitting his dog to ruin his bushes and plants when actually Charles' dog was always tied up, on leash, or in the house. Nothing Charles said or did seemed to help. The work of neighborhood dogs was always blamed on his dog.

Charles decided to convince his neighbor with psychotronic energy and came to me for instruction. He was ready to start after the first lesson and chose a beautiful sunset as his psychotronic scene. He saw himself talking with his neighbor and pointing out other dogs as they trespassed on his property, doing what the man had accused his dog of doing.

He pointed at the imaged dogs. He held eye contact with the

imaged neighbor. He felt understanding for the error, forgiveness, rapport.

It did not take two days to work. The neighbor came over the second morning as Charles was opening his garage. He said he had been mistaken, and wanted to apologize. He brought a large soup bone for the dog. He and Charles have been good neighbors and friends ever since.

Can you imagine seeing a sunset together with the tyrant in your life? Then start with that.

Here are some other scenes that you may wish to progress through as you repeat the Action Plan working toward the sending of true love—and the "death" of a tyrant.

- Talking to a third party together
- Having a drink together
- Having a meal together
- Shaking hands
- Forgiving each other
- Embracing

Action plan to stop a tyrant

Go to your "special room" under the skylight and relax deeply.

Fill the room with a blue light.

Invite the tyrant in, and see the tyrant mellow in the blue light.

Create a scene that you can tolerate, as described above, changing to a more and more harmonious scene each time you repeat the Action Plan.

Move closer to the tyrant, imagining that you are holding eye contact.

Send your loving thoughts.

End your session.

THE MAGIC SHIELD THAT PROTECTS YOU FROM PSYCHIC ATTACK

Sometimes you are victimized by a person you would least expect, and in a way you would never discover.

Take Mrs. Emma P. She was thirty years younger than her husband, a gentleman farmer. Emma began to have recurrent headaches and was always tired. She could hardly do the housework. Each morning she would see her husband off to the fields he tended with a crew of workers and then she would collapse. At the end of the day, he would return vigorous for his advanced years while she was still in a state of depletion and pain.

After months of this she sought assistance from the author. I went to my special room and played back a typical day. I saw her husband feeding on her energy. Even though she was in the house and he was hundreds of yards away, he was "siphoning" energy from her.

I ended my session and told her what I saw, being careful to explain that this was not a conscious act on her husband's part but merely a byproduct of his love of her and dependence on her, and that many people are unwittingly the victims of psychic "vampires."

She was lucky, I explained. Oft times it is not burglarizing of energy but bombardment with energy—all negative.

I gave her the following Action Plan to do immediately, and ushered her into a room where she could relax in privacy:

Action plan to halt psychic attack

Relax quietly, eyes closed, breathing rhythmically, feeling safe.

Picture a plastic bubble around you. It is impenetrable except by the highest vibrational energy, like light and love.

See human attack, conscious or unconscious, bouncing off this bubble and returning to sender, as you end your session.

Renew this plastic bubble daily.

Emma emerged from the room a few minutes later. Her headache had ended the moment she installed the plastic bubble.

You can use this method for any kind of psychic attack. The trick is to be aware of this kind of malpractice. Here are some symptoms to watch for:

- Unexplained nervousness or feelings of impending trouble
- Fatigue, headache, insomnia
- Morbid feelings, depression, excessive pessimism
- Persistent recurrence of an ailmanet—cough, back pains, gout, arthritis, etc.

Although these are not conclusive signs of psychic attack—they could be due to any number of physical factors and should first be treated by a physician—they do occur frequently in psychic cases.

HOW TO CHANGE OBNOXIOUS ATTITUDES IN OTHER PEOPLE

Most behavior, good or bad, is conditioned. We learn to be the way we are. This learning or conditioning then becomes automatic, like typing or riding a bicyle.

The Russian scientist Pavlov discovered that if he rang a bell every time he fed his dogs, soon just by ringing the bell the dogs' saliva would begin to flow.

Behavioral psychologists use this principle today to help their clients change unwanted conditionings or habits—like smoking or overeating. A system of rewards and punishments (including an electric shock every time the smoker lights up) soon changes the habit.

This principle works using psychotronic energy as well—the energy of consciousness.

A university class worked this once on their professor. He had the habit of pacing across the room from one side to the other. The students conspired to give him their attention on the left side but not on the right side. Within one period he stopped his pacing and was teaching from the left side.

The energy of human consciousness has been shown to affect other types of life. In an experiment using Kirlian photography, the radiations of a leaf were altered in several ways, according to a technical paper delivered at the Second World Psychotronic Conference in Monte Carlo. A man sent his thoughts to the leaf in the sense of "my will against yours" and succeeded in causing a minor contraction in the leaf's aura. A woman visualized a plastic bubble around the leaf restricting the aura. She too succeeded in obtaining measurable results.

If you combine these two facts:

1. Psychotronic energy can condition
2. Conditioning can change behavior

Then you see how your own thoughts can change another person's habitual ways.

There is an advantage to psychotronic energy as a conditioning force. It transcends physical obstacles and works on higher principles.

Let's say Joe L. is an obnoxious character. You have to work with

Joe and it is proving to be a problem. If you were to have a talk with Joe, it would probably only make matters worse. On the other hand, when you go to Joe in your imagination, things are different on this conscious level. Joe wants to improve. He wants to be loved like we all do. The problem is he is conditioned to be the way he is. His higher consciousness–superconscious, if you will–would be glad to make a change for the better were it possible.

You can make it possible. Here is how.

You can "see" Joe able to talk more and more reasonably every time he drinks a cup of coffee. You know he drinks coffee, so "see" him changing for the better with every sip of the hot coffee that he takes.

These are triggering devices, just like the Pavlov bells, only on a psychotronic level. You could use tea or water or beer. Or you could use putting on his shirt as a triggering device, or stepping on the foot pedal of his car. Anything he does occasionally which you can picture him doing is workable.

You cannot trigger a person to behave in a negative way. Only improvements are possible. This is because Joe really wants to improve, as any person does. There is resistance to motion in the other direction. Conditioning sent with psychotronic energy works only for human betterment.

Here is your Action Plan.

Action plan to transform an obnoxious person

Relax in your "special room."

Invite the obnoxious person to join you.

See the person becoming less and less obnoxious with every sip of coffee or other triggering device.

Know that your psychotronic energy is conditioning new behavior in this person.

Visualize the person changing for the better with each repetition of the triggering action.

End your session, expecting a change, and feeling a change for the better in your own attitude toward the person.

HOW TO MAKE A PERSON SHAPE UP FAST

Shouts of delight are coming from the gymnasium. One of the youngsters has pinned a photograph of the school principal on the dart board and now each of the group of students is taking a "shot" at him.

Even if he is unaware of what is going on, the principal is experiencing moments of unpleasantness, which he cannot explain. What the students do not understand, though, is that they are only making the principal harder to get along with and harder on them.

The energy of consciousness generates its own kind. Hate begets hate. Love begets love.

Therefore it is psychotronic love that solves human problems. There is no faster way to get a person to shape up than by bombarding him with psychotronic love.

There is a way that this is done with the eyes and hands working together that makes a person shape up so fast it takes your breath away.

You need some materials: a photograph of the person, or a realistic sketch; some flowers or pictures in color of flowers; incense, or perfume, a candle; a record, with spiritual or romantic music, preferably without voices.

In addition, some other art materials will be useful, since you are going to be creating a paste-up or montage. These could include crayons or colored chalk, cotton, and things like tinsel or decorative paper.

You also need a large piece of cardboard, or heavy paper to use as backing. You may also do this directly on a wall, being careful not to use materials that will take paint off or create permanent stains. The backing will need to be posted on a wall for best results.

The first step is to post the photograph of the person you wish to make shape up in the center of the backing or wall space. Draw a triangle around it with the apex up. Next, surround it with flowers, real or in picture form. In addition, create designs by chalk or crayon indicating yellow sunbursts around the person and within the sunbursts a blue halo or aura, the darker blue the better.

Add any other decorative material to your montage that will give it sparkle, radiance, or color. Position a floor lamp or table lamp in such a way that it illuminates the montage like a spotlight.

You are now ready to begin the Action Plan.

Action plan to make a pesky person shape up fast

Stand, facing the montage.

Close your eyes and know that when you next open them, you will be in your special room still facing the montage but the person will be "real."

Open your eyes gazing into the eyes of the person.

Feel love for the person.

Understand his problems and be thankful they are not your problems.

Send him psychotronic love energy with your eyes and hands, lifting both arms and reaching the fingers of both hands toward the person. Use a finger position of cupped hands beckoning.

Hold eye contact with the person and maintain the finger position for several minutes, all the while feeling the love that comes with complete understanding.

Make caressing motions with your hands, expressing affection.

End your session knowing that the power of love has transformed the person, as it indeed will prove to do.

George L. was involved in a traffic accident in which a young man riding in the car George was driving was killed. George was overcome with remorse but felt it was the fault of the other driver. Instead, charges were filed against him and he was scheduled for a court appearance.

George worried about a prison sentence that would ruin his life. He saw all of his dreams of a successful career about to end in disgrace.

When he was given procedures for preventing this tragedy, he jumped at the opportunity and became a proficient relaxer and visualizer.

George knew what the judge looked like and sketched him. Then he created a mural around the sketch composed of Indian art or mandalas. Then he went through the action plan. When he made his court appearance, the judge showed a great compassion and the charges were dismissed.

GEOMETRIC SHAPES AND FORMS THAT AFFECT PEOPLE

The reason for drawing a triangle around the picture in this last Action Plan has to do with the effect of symbols on our consciousness. Some geometric shapes have deep significance which our consciousness reacts to even if we are not aware of the inner meaning of that shape.

A circle is a symbol of unity. It has a good affect on consciousness by tending to remind an individual that his apparently separate mind is really part of a large universal mind.

A triangle is also a significant symbol that triggers a positive conscious effect, especially in the direction of balancing out things when they are out of balance.

The three tips of the triangle are conceived as intelligence, love, and force. When these three qualities are in perfect balance, we ourselves are in perfect balance and perform in god-like ways, expressing the perfection of God in our thoughts and activities.

Now that's really shaping up! If you can move a person from being obnoxious to expressing god-like qualities, you are going as far as you can in changing a problem to a solution.

In Christianity, the triangle symbolizes Father, Mother, Son—the Triune aspects of the Creator, with the Father, Divine Will (force); the Mother, the Holy Spirit (wisdom or intelligence) and the Son, Jesus the Lord whom men call the Christ (love).

The brain is divided into two hemispheres. The right side of the brain, which controls the left side of the body, is "in charge of" pictures. The left side of the brain, which controls the right side of the body is "in charge of" words.

Canadian scientists have perfected a way of balancing the two hemispheres of the brain, and thus enhancing the health and functioning of the person, by a system of drawing pictures and describing these pictures verbally—a system they call Eidetic Biofeedback.

Members of the Canadian Academy of Psychotronics have been active in researching how different geometric shapes affect different people, recognizing that consciousness is energy—force—motion, constantly seeking to express itself in form, pattern and symbol. They have found that a shape of package or design of package will change a person's taste experience of the food within it. The same food in a differently designed package produces a different taste.

The research is being extended to cover the effect of different shaped rooms and buildings on the creative work within those buildings.

Of course, these same shapes projected mentally from one person to another have the same effects as when perceived through the senses.

In the author's experience, the square, rectangle, trapezoid and irregular shapes have from a negative to a neutral reaction, whereas the following shapes or symbols transmitted in an Action Plan, psychotronically, have a neutral to a positive influence:

Cross
Star
Triangle
Circle
Dot

How to enhance the effects of any action plan with geometry symbols

Perform your action plan as directed.

Insert the symbol, above or around the person when you will call him or her into your special room.

Decorate your "special room" with that symbol in a number of places.

COLORS AFFECT PEOPLE AND HOW YOU CAN USE CERTAIN COLORS TO INFLUENCE OTHERS

Kirlian Photography now confirms what psychics have known for millennia–the human body radiates energy and this energy when conceived visually has color characteristics.

The energy fields around people's fingers, for instance, show a response to the mental stance at the moment. A man and a woman may show greenish blue "auras" around their finger tips, but when they touch the colors shift toward the reds and oranges.

Psychologists have found that people's color preference gives insight into their personality. Retailers have found that people respond more to certain colored lights and displays than to others. Color therapy is being used to correct certain health problems.

Color and consciousness are in communication with each other and it is two-way. Consciousness produces colors and colors affect consciousness.

Recently I had a very low attendance in a course I teach at a local university. Since the course is advertised by bulletin and flyer, the next time the course was offered, I surrounded the printed material with red light before it was distributed. That time the turn-out tripled.

You can use color to control people. You merely bathe the

person in the right colored light in your imagination. The person is affected by the color and the tendency to respond is increased.

Here are the colors to use:

Red When you want to make physical love or create an emotional reaction.

Orange When you want to be with the person at a party or influence the person's role in a group of people, club, or organization.

Green When you want to make a sale or create a more tranquil and harmonious relationship.

Blue When you want to make a person friendly and comfortable.

Indigo When you want to bring out the highest in a person.

Here is how you use color in your Action Plans.

Action plan to use color to "move" a person

Go to your special room by closing your eyes and relaxing.

Install indirect color lighting in your special room with controls in the arm of your chair, a button for each color.

Any time you invite a person into your special room for a particular Action Plan turn on the color appropriate to that action.

See the person bathed in that special color light.

Scientists are recognizing the importance of full spectrum light to total health. Window panes that cut out ultra-violet rays, eye glasses that cut out portions of the spectrum, and artificial light that supplies only a portion of the spectrum are now being examined as prime sources of mental and physical problems. Full spectrum glass and eyeglasses are now being made available.

A special color light properly chosen can add a color that has been in short supply. It helps to correct and normalize.

Light and psychotronic energy are very closely related. The eyes are the organs of both.

WORKING WITH YOUR EYES IN THE PERSON OF A BULLY

It is best to operate against bullies, tyrants and obnoxious people on a subjective level–when you are relaxed and can utilize your imaging faculty at a distance from them.

But should the occasion arise, you can use your psychotronic energy in person with instant effects.

Patricia P. was caring on a part-time basis for an emotionally disturbed boy—a teenager quite tall for his age. She had taken the lad for a walk to nearby fields, and they had climbed a grassy hill when a thunderstorm approached. The boy became agitated. He seemed to blame Patricia for every flash of lightning and roll of thunder. Suddenly he turned toward Patricia and stalked toward her, face grimaced and hands reaching out as if to choke her.

Patricia kept cool and unmoved. She knew the miracle of psychotronic power. She opened her eye apertures to a pronounced stare, held eye contact with the crazed youth as he approached, saw him enveloped in a blue light, and felt love and understanding for him.

Six inches from her neck, his hands dropped and he spun around as if in shame. She took his arm and led him back home.

Opening the eye aperture commands attention and magnifies the psychotronic energy transmitted. This is often used as a hypnotic technique but that is a different approach which takes special skill and training.

You are able to use the psychotronic approach without any more skill or training than you are given in this book—safely and effectively.

Use the wide eyed technique but not to command hypnotically, instead to control psychotronically with the super-weapon: love.

When another person threatens you, use this Action Plan.

Action plan to quiet a bully face to face

Open your eyes slightly wider than the normal, careful not to put a horror expression on your face, instead . . .

Keep your face expressionless. Do not smile.

See a blue light enveloping the person.

Feel love, sympathy, rapport and understanding.

Magnify those feelings by turning them up as if with an imaginary rheostat.

Transmit those feelings with your eyes.

In the next chapter, you learn how to use your hands to help other people improve their mental and physical well-being in ways that have opened the eyes of the medical profession to new frontiers of the mind.

6

PSYCHOTRONIC POWER FOR IMPROVED HEALTH AND WELL BEING OF OTHERS

In this chapter you learn to use your hands to massage your loved ones in a healing way. You learn to detect health problems in other people and conduct psychotronic healing sessions for them. You can stop a spouse from snoring or a child from wetting the bed. Four simple requirements are all that are needed. In this chapter there are techniques for enhancing each of these four requirements in yourself for greater healing power. Finally, there is a method to use the sun to reinforce vigorous health by way of optical psychotronic energy.

The power in your hands will be brought into greater play in this chapter. You will be able to create profound change for the better in other people with proper application of psychotronic energy, aided by your hands.

About a century ago, a young man named Tom Fisher was to be hanged at Carbon County Prison in Jim Thorpe, Pennsylvania. The night before, he placed his right hand on the wall of the cell and vowed that this mark would remain on that wall as long as the prison stood, as a sign of his innocence.

Today, that handprint remains. No matter what is done to wash or paint over it, the erie handprint reappears–testimony to the miraculous power of psychotronic energy especially when focused through the hands.

But what is an even greater testimony to this power, is its acceptance by prestigious scientific resources. This is not only its greatest testimony but its greatest promise. For what you are able to do through the Action Plans in this book, miraculous as they appear, are only minor accomplishments compared to what science will make possible through their investigation of psychotronic power.

The highly respected Smithsonian Institution has compiled a traveling exhibit dealing with psychic phenomenon. The exhibit is being sent to colleges, universities, museums and libraries throughout the United States and Canada.

It includes scientifically proven cases of psychic healing, psychokinesis (moving objects with psychotronic energy), precognition, mental telepathy and others, including the ESP experiments conducted at Stanford Research Institute, dowsing, and psychic criminal investigation.

We might call this Smithsonian exhibit official recognition that mankind has entered a new age–an age of the use of the energy of consciousness we call psychotronic power.

HOW TO USE YOUR MIND, HANDS AND EYES TO SEND HEALING ENERGY THROUGH THE PERSON YOU TOUCH

Although the energy of consciousness knows no limitations of space and time that other energies must overcome, it can still be applied *here* and now quite effectively compared to physical energies.

In Chapter 4 we gave you the introduction to health improvements using your psychotronic energy. In this chapter we go into more specific steps to head off, alleviate, and dissolve mental and physical health problems.

Psychic surgeons of the Philippines were recently visited by some scientific observers who were interested in whether these so-called psychic surgeons really had the power in their hands to reach through skin and pull out tumors, cysts, and other growths.

They observed, saw what purported to be exactly that but had no way to be absolutely sure they were not being fooled. However, they did discover one indisputable piece of evidence that pointed to special powers: The psychic surgeons could point their fingers at dental x-ray film and cause images to appear!

You have this same power in your hands. All you need to do is activate it and you have already begun this process.

A reminder that you are not becoming a physician. You are becoming a psychic healer. A physician may use psychic healing methods and frequently does, intentionally or unintentionally. But a psychic healer may never use a physician's methods. It is against the law.

It is against the law to diagnose an illness and to prescribe or treat for that illness. Psychic healers do not run afoul of this law when they do their work secretly and at a distance.

In this chapter we will remain secret but some of the things we will do will be in the person's presence, and even touching that person, in the nature of laying on of hands as done in faith healing and moving the hands over the person as done in massage.

Touching and massaging is legally acceptable among members of your own family, but you may need to get legal advice as to the proper procedure in your state for extending this teatment beyond the members of your immediate family.

Healing energy is surging through you as you read this book. It is stronger now than it was on page one, because you are more aware of your capabilities.

If you see yourself as a separate unit, you become more separated from this energy. If you see yourself as part of universal conscious, as connected to a Cosmic Psychotronic Generator, you act more as a conductor, or channel, for this energy.

American Indians who felt close to nature, so close they were indeed "one" with nature, had great healing energy. If an Indian was ill, he went to a "medicine man." This Indian healer took a walk in the fields or woods. In his consciousness he projected the question to nature, "What will cure this person?"

He was then attracted to a bark, root, herb or leaf. It was as if that living thing was answering him.

Today we know that plants communicate both with each other and with man. This communication has been monitored by the polygraph, or lie detector equipment.

The Indian medicine man "heard" this reply. It is equivalent to a higher power leading him to the cure he sought.

Soloho, a Hopi healer, still gets information to heal his people, and others who come to him, by this type of communication. He is also able to attune his consciousness to this higher power and place his hands on an ailing body in such a way as to bring the ailing parts additional life energy. Sometimes his hands began to move over the body in a massaging manner to reach tissues, ligaments, glands, and organs that need additional psychotronic energy.

This is not a monopoly. Just about every culture has its healing methods through massage, or the laying on of hands.

Every person has this ability. The more he is convinced of this fact, the better it works for him.

You have this ability. It works for you. Here is how:

Action plan to heal by massage

Ask an ailing member of your family if they would like your assistance by massage.

Instruct the person to lie face down.

Sit astride the person.

Relax and go to your "special room" under the skylight.

See yourself and the person bathed in green light.

Move your hands over the body gently permitting them to go where they seem to want to go, and stay where they want to stay.

Keep your mind on the skylight as you continue this process for several minutes.

Repeat with the person on his or her back.

End the session knowing help has been given.

Sarah L.'s back hurt. It had constant pain in the lower portion. Her husband urged her to see their doctor, but Sarah preferred to rest and hope for the best.

One evening, when her husband returned from work and found no dinner and the bed unmade, he decided to try and help using his knowledge of psychotronic power. Sarah agreed to a massage, but her husband just held his hands on her lower back, first here then there. In ten minutes, the pain was gone and did not return.

OFFICIAL RECOGNITION NOW GIVEN TO HEALING POWER OF PSYCHOTRONIC ENERGY

In early days religions were the domain of healing work. As medical science emerged, religious healing began to fade. Now it is called psychic healing, or faith healing, and only a few churches still include it in their activities.

However, a new phase is underway. Medical science is discovering faith healing. More precisely, psychotronics is opening the door of conscious energy to medicine.

Research into the effects of psychotronic energy transfers between animals and plants has been done in the Soviet Union that showed a reaction in plants to the death of animals and other specific indications of energy transfers.

In Japan, researchers at the Institute for Religious Psychology have measured human energy radiation from both the body's chakra points of yoga and its meridian points of acupuncture.

Barta Carol, a psychiatrist with Nucet Hospital in Romania, has been studying the bio-atom and bio-electromagnetic energy as a key to health.

One psychic healer after another is being frankly and unabashedly examined by scientists and physicians both in the laboratory and in the healing situation.

Kirlian photography is being utilized by psychiatrists and psychologists as a possible aid in diagnosing mental illness.

PSYCHIC "DIAGNOSIS" AT A DISTANCE

You can perfect your own natural ability to detect abnormalities in a person.

When you have a sincere desire to help somebody, your mind resonates with every molecule in that person no matter where that person is.

He or she could be thousands of miles away but your mind transcends distance just the way light does and maybe faster and easier.

Remember, I said "a sincere desire." The desire to show somebody you can do it, is not a sincere desire to heal. The desire to put on a demonstration or make a name for yourself is not a sincere desire.

The desire of a parent to help a child is most likely a sincere desire. But the further away the relationship, the more likely that pollutants can affect the sincerity.

Examine your motive. If it is free of side issues and focused entirely on helping the other person to health with no thought of reward or recognition for yourself, you are passing the test of sincerity.

That means you are attuned accurately and can detect in a dependable way. Here is how:

Action plan to detect the nature of illness in another person and help them

Go to your "special room" under the skylight and mentally invite the person to join you.

Examine the person by scanning his body up and down until your attention is called to any one or two parts.

Focus your attention on the first of these parts.

Snap your fingers to make the detail larger and brighter.

Ask the part what is wrong with it. The next thought that pops into your mind is quite likely the answer.

Make a mental correction of the illness or abnormality in the person's body.

Use your hands to "fix" it.

Do the same for the second part of the body, and even a third if there is one.

End your session.

Thousands of men and women, even children, all over the world are able to do this as a result of just a few hours of training. The author has personally trained hundreds who are successful psychotronic "diagnosticians." This training is largely a matter of reprogramming the subconscious mind from "I can't do it" to "I can do it."

Actually, they are warned not to diagnose. This is against the medical laws. What they are really doing is detecting health problems at a distance.

Nor are they healers. What they are really doing when they "fix" is making corrections at a nonphysical, or spiritual, level—again at a distance.

Sam G. was taking his medical exams. The strain was getting to him. He felt weak and had spells of dizziness. He knew enough about the nervous system to understand that his physical symptoms were the result of nervous tension. He asked a fellow graduate of Silva Mind Control, one of several commercial courses that train this skill, to help him strengthen his nerves and correct the physical imbalance.

"It's urgent," he said, "Every hour counts between now and the exams."

The psychotronic healer waited till Sam left. He then went to his "special room," saw Sam in his imagination, gave him an imaginary injection of a new product he invented on the spot called "Instant Nerve Strengthener and Self-Confidence Reinforcer."

Sam later reported that his weakness and dizziness had never re-occurred. He felt more competent when he took his exams, free of any nervousness. And he passed.

Laura B. was in her bedroom when she heard a familiar wheezing sound. Her 11-year-old son was having an asthma attack. It could be another sleepless night. Without leaving her bed, she visited him in her imagination, administered an imaginary relaxer, and waited. In less than a minute the attack was over.

HOW TO END CRYING TANTRUMS IN CHILDREN

A child is crying.

He tells his mother there is a monster in his room. He is afraid to go to sleep.

"Where, Tommy?"

His mother looks in the closet. Gets down and peers under the bed.

"There's no monster, Tommy. It's your imagination. Now go to sleep."

She turns out the light.

"It's there, Mom. On the ceiling. Can't you see it? Above the window. Mom, don't let it eat me!"

"I don't see it, Tommy. Now you pretend it isn't there. If it causes any trouble, I'll send your father in to help you."

She leaves and goes into the living room where her husband is chatting with me, a neighbor.

"Tommy sees a monster in his room. I told him you're the monster killer. But wait, he'll probably fall asleep."

Tommy cries again. His father goes in to see him. There is quiet for a few minutes, but as soon as his father returns to the living room, Tommy begins all over. His crying now has escalated to screaming.

"Some monster-killer you are," taunts Mom.

"Do you mind if I try to help?" I ask.

"Be our guest," says Dad, "The light switch is on the right as you enter."

"No," I reply, "I'll work right in this chair."

Now Mom and Dad look at each other.

I change to a more comfortable position, close my eyes, and take three deep breaths. In a minute I open my eyes.

"He'll be okay now. Give him a minute."

The screaming continues. Then it tapers off to sobs. Then they seem to hear Tommy laugh. Then there is quiet.

"What in the world did you do?"

I explain subjective programming.

"If Tommy was handled objectively, he could be reasoned with, or he could be asked certain questions that would reveal the anxiety that was causing the 'monster.' He could even be programmed with positive statements to give up the monster.

"But it's much easier programming Tommy subjectively. To do this the programmer needs to go to a deep mental level, sort of turning off the outside physical world. I do this often. Once there, I saw Tommy in his bed. I also saw the monster. Believe me, it was every bit as terrifying as Tommy claimed.

"I then saw Tommy screaming and with each scream, I 'made' the monster diminish in size until after just a few more screams it was just a toy monster. I 'talked' to Tommy and 'told' him it was just a toy monster. Then I ended my mental level knowing it was taken care of."

And so it was.

Psychotronics works just as well stopping your spouse from snoring or your child from wetting his bed or yourself from smoking or over-eating.

It works just as well getting a job, a raise, or a promotion.

It works getting rid of your or other people's health problems.

It works eliminating animosities, hostilities, or friction—among others, or yourself and others.

It works getting rid of financial problems, political problems, social problems.

All you need is that sincere desire.

A DOCTOR USES ENERGY OF CONSCIOUSNESS SUCCESSFULLY IN CANCER THERAPY

A woman has cancer throughout her body. It has gone into her brain and into her bones. She cannot walk. When she tries to eat, she bites her tongue because of the effects on her brain and nerve system.

Carl Simonton, M.D., recently described this case, one of many, in a talk to the Academy of Parapsychology and Medicine, outlining some of the techniques in his practice as a radiologist at Travis Air Force. The results were a far greater percentage of remissions and cures and in a much shorter time.

The woman was quite cooperative and enthusiastic about helping in her own cure, Dr. Simonton relates. She had a strong religious background and saw spiritual implications in the procedures. Within a week of applying these procedures she was walking with assistance, and eating. Within two weeks she was essentially off all pain medication and went home.

"It was one of the most dramatic recoveries I have ever seen," recalls Dr. Simonton. And he has seen many while practicing at Travis and privately in Texas where he is now.

However, when this woman went home, she was returning to the source of her cancer. Hers was a hostile marriage and friction was the order of the day.

In a month she was dead.

I select this case as an introduction to the technique Dr. Simonton uses so as to temper any false hopes with an understanding of cause and effect in mind-body relationships. I am sure Dr. Simonton includes this among the many dramatic successes he illustrates his discussions with for the same essential reason.

Many cases remain free of the disease. At least symptoms do not return. He hesitates to use the word "cure."

What is the technique? It is basically this:

1. The patient is shown slides of previous patients—before and after pictures showing the disappearance of the disease. This

helps to overcome mental attitudes of defeatism and to establish an attitude of optimism and expectancy.

2. The patient is taught to relax using largely the method previously described, and then going to a mental "peaceful place." The patient is asked to do this three times for fifteen minutes each time, morning, noon and night.
3. The family is asked to do likewise on their own. (Removing the cause?)
4. Once relaxed, the patient is asked to picture his cancer in any way he sees it. This need not bear any direct relation to normal anatomy. Anyway the patient sees it, that makes sense to him, is all right.
5. Then, as the last step, he sees the treatment working. If that treatment is radiation, he sees the beam of x-ray of energy bullets entering his body, hitting all the cells. He sees the normal cells repairing their damage, the cancer cells unable to and dying. He sees the white blood cells–the body's defense system–picking up and getting rid of the dead and dying cancer cells.

That's all there is to it. The patient ends his relaxation and mental picturing and goes about his normal activities.

Sound familiar? It is using the alpha level of mind to activate psychotronic energy for aiding your own health problem.

A doctor is proving it works.

It works not only on cancer. It works on any abnormality. Expectation and belief are an essential factor. They are just as essential as the relaxing and visualizing procedures.

It works permanently only if the original cause of the abnormality is identified and inhibited or removed. Getting the whole family to relax, too, and visualize a peaceful place and a cure taking place is a good back-up procedure. If they have a "that's ridiculous" attitude toward the sick person's relaxing and visualizing, they are in effect, working against it. By understanding and cooperating they assist. And then there's always the possibility that family friction is the cause and that relaxation and positive imaging can "take the sting out."

Little Peter L., 4, had a big stomach. Other children in his prekindergarten class called him fatty. What they did not know was Peter had kidney trouble. His body was bloated with toxins. The doctor said it was irreversible. It was just a matter of time before

Peter would have to be put on a kidney machine periodically for the rest of his life.

Peter's mother knew the power of the mind. The author coached her on how to apply her psychotronic energy in this case. She was to go to her special room, see her son, and go inside his kidneys waking up all the cells. She was also to explain to Peter to imagine he was doing the same things. "Wake up every part of your kidneys," she instructed Peter, and Peter agreed.

Four days later Peter's stomach was normal. The doctor said it was an unexplained remission. Peter said, "I woke my kidneys up. I'm not fat anymore. His mother called me and said "Thanks." I said, "I didn't do it. You and Peter did."

HOW TO HELP YOUR OWN BODY PSYCHOTRONICALLY TO CORRECT ITS MALFUNCTIONS

Back in 1866 Mary Baker Eddy, herself healed in a nonmedical way, founded Christian Science. Based metaphysically on the total acceptance of the concept of perfection, one might say that Christian Science was one of the first to use the power of consciousness in a positive, constructive way toward the betterment of health.

Today, psychotronic scientists, and, in a way, Dr. Carl Simonton is one such scientist, are discovering the value of that concept of perfection. They find that:

The image of perfection, held confidently at the relaxed level of mind, has the power to change imperfection.

Let's examine components of the above statement:

Image
Perfection
Confidence
Relaxed

These are four equally essential requirements. Without all four the secret formula for self-healing is incomplete.

Can you see yourself when you close your eyes?
Can you see yourself free of the illness, abnormality or affliction that you may have?
Are you confident in the power of your mind to make you sick and to make you well?

Are you able to relax your body and mind deeply while confidently picturing yourself perfect?

If the answer is no to any one of these, then you need to work on it. Here are exercises you can do. First—to see yourself with your eyes closed.

Action plan to visualize yourself more realistically

Stand in front of a full length mirror without clothes on. (Nudity should be considered as your doctor considers it.)

Look at yourself head to toe slowly, starting with your hair.

See how the hair is combed, the wrinkles on your forehead, the complexion of your face.

Re-examine and rediscover your features, your physical shape, your assets and liabilities all the way down to your toes.

Close your eyes and review your looks again.

Repeat several times.

Next—to see yourself perfect, when you are having some difficulty doing so—it is helpful to have a photo of yourself taken before the physical problem began. If it is an overweight problem, find a picture of yourself in younger and lighter years. If it is lack of energy, find a picture of yourself when you were as active as you would like to be once again. If you have no such photograph available, conjure it up in your mind's eye. Imagine yourself being photographed. See the imaginary photo as it would appear.

Bring your photograph, imagined or on paper, into this action plan:

Action plan to better visualize yourself as you wish to be

Relax in a comfortable chair.

Close your eyes and see yourself perfect.

Improve your concept of perfection by bringing the photo or imagined photo into your line of vision.

Open your eyes without disturbing your relaxation and see or "see" the picture of yourself.

Close your eyes and see yourself perfect as in that picture.

Repeat several times.

End your relaxation.

Now, if you need to reinforce your confidence, the repetition of positive affirmations will strengthen this critical factor:

Action plan to strengthen confidence in self-healing ability

Relax deeply.

Go to your "special room."

Notice the skylight above you.

Feel your oneness with the universe.

Repeat several times mentally, "I am one with the perfect universe. Health is my natural state. I invite and accept perfect health. My mind is the servant of universal perfection."

End your session. Repeat occasionally.

You are now ready to cement the final span in your bridge to health—deep relaxation.

HOW TO ATTAIN AN EVEN DEEPER STATE OF RELAXATION FOR GREATER PSYCHOTRONIC POWER

Some people can relax at will.

For others, the very idea of relaxing causes them to tense up.

Psychotronic power works best when you are really and truly relaxed, when you are at the alpha level of mind which is seven to fourteen electrical pulsations per second. Mid-way—10½ pulsations—is also the mid-way point between zero and 21, the average high point of most people. At this mid-point the mind seems to encompass both aspects of its dual functioning—physical and nonphysical.

To relax more deeply than you are currently relaxing when you implement an Action Plan is to invite greater success. Even if you believe you have no problem in this department, take time to improve in the following way.

Select five of the following methods to enhance relaxation, the five that you are most comfortable with:

1. Tense your jaws. Let go. Feel the sense of relief at that moment. Capture that sense. Tense your feet. Let go. Cap-

ture the sense of letting go, exactly what it feels like. Spread that feeling throughout your body.

2. Stare at a point above the normal line of sight. Keep head straight, eyes turned upward. When your eyes feel like blinking, permit them to close.
3. Take three deep breaths. As you exhale the first time, imagine it is the end of the day, and it feels so good to relax; with the second exhalation, feel a wave of relaxation going from head to toe; with the third exhalation, feel yourself getting heavier in the chair.
4. Repeat over and over "I am getting heavier and heavier as I let go. Heavier and heavier as I relax."
5. Repeat over and over "I am getting sleepier and sleepier with every passing moment."
6. Sit quietly with eyes closed, being aware of your breathing. Know that with every rhythmic breath you take you are getting more and more deeply relaxed.
7. Count backwards from 25 to one, feeling yourself going deeper with each count.
8. Imagine you are a mine elevator and the elevator is descending deeper and deeper into the mine.
9. Imagine you are on the top floor of a large department store. The elevator stops at each floor as it descends and there is a taped announcement as to what is on each floor. Finally it reaches the bargain basement.
10. Be aware of your scalp. Relax all tissues and tiny muscles. Do the same with your forehead, eyes, cheeks, jaw, mouth, neck, shoulders, arms and so forth, all the way down to your toes. Take your time.
11. Take a deep breath, and as you exhale, give yourself the instructions, "Relax more deeply *now.*"
12. Imagine you are in your bed. You are very comfortable. It is quiet and peaceful. You are about to fall asleep.
13. Imagine you are in a flower garden. You admire the blossoms. You hold one in your hand. There is a drop of water on it reflecting all the colors of the rainbow. See the colors, the jewel-like beauty.
14. Imagine you are lying on a beach, listening to the surf or in a grassy meadow looking up at the slowly drifting billowy white clouds.
15. Count backwards very slowly from ten to one. Allow about ten seconds between each count, knowing that when you get to one, you are deeply relaxed.

Once you have selected the five that come most naturally to you—with which you feel most agreeable and comfortable—then do them in the order that they appear.

You might want to write them on five cards numbered in the proper order, one to five. You can open your eyes during your relaxation session and look at the next card. It will not disturb your relaxation. Or, you may want to use a word or two to trigger your memory as to what the step is—like "countdown" or "department store."

This is all part of your preparation for this next Action Plan to relax more deeply and effectively. One more step in this preparation is to select a secret word that you will use to trigger instant relaxation in the future.

Your secret word will act to trigger the same deep relaxation again that you are about to attain now. You will not have to go through this Action Plan more than once. All you will need to do is say your secret word.

This word can be any word. It can be as short as "now" as long as "antidisestablishmentarianism" as common as "relax" as uncommon as "Rumpelstiltskin." Should anybody else say it to you it will have no effect on you. When you say it, it will.

Do you have your secret word? And the five steps selected? Then proceed as follows:

Action plan for instant alpha mind relaxation

Sit comfortably in a straight-back chair.

Proceed to follow the five selected procedures in their numbered order. When the fifth is completed . . .

Repeat mentally several times, "I can attain this deep, healthful state of relaxation, any time in the future, by merely saying this word" (say mentally your secret word.)

Remind yourself that when you count to three you will feel wide awake, full of energy, and at a high level of well-being and enthusiasm.

Count to three.

Open your eyes.

SELF-HEALING WITH YOUR OWN PSYCHOTRONIC POWER

With your enhanced ability to image yourself perfect while deeply relaxed and supremely confident, you are ready to focus your own energy of consciousness for the correction of your body's health abnormalities.

Some see this as a type of meditation.

Others see it as similar to prayer.

Don't deny either.

We do not know enough about the energy we call psychotronic or the workings of prayer to say that they are mutually inclusive or mutually exclusive.

At this point in his evolution, man needs to keep all philosophical and spiritual options open.

There are some advantages in considering this psychotronic healing as connected with spiritual healing or prayer. Such concepts are more universal. By accepting a concept that acknowledges your playing a part in something bigger than you, there is an automatic "hooking up" with the Cosmic Psychotronic Generator.

You have worked hard to reach this moment. You deserve a simple Action Plan. And it is:

Action plan to heal yourself

Go to your "special room" under the skylight.

Say your secret word to relax deeply.

Invite yourself into the room as if you had a second self.

See the physical problem.

Correct the physical problem with your hands, mending, sewing, normalizing, using imaginary germ killers, tumor shrinkers, blood pressure normalizers, or whatever you can invent mentally to do the job.

Imagine yourself perfect, holding that image a minute or more.

End your session knowing a cure is activated.

Prepare to accept it.

You are a different person, physically, with every passing second. Cells are being born to replace dying cells. After this Action Plan, new cells are being born to fit your image of perfection.

Bernard R. was told by his physician that he had a hernia—an opening in the abdominal wall into which his intestines would sink and become constricted. A truss would be only a temporary aid. An operation was the only solution, he was told.

Bernard decided he would help his body correct this abnormality. Every night he performed the above Action Plan. He raised his intestines and closed the abdominal gap. He "applied" a hardening and toughening agent to strengthen the abdominal wall. It took just one minute, before falling asleep.

In three months he returned for another physical exam. His doctor looked surprised. "It's still there," he said, "but there has been no progression. In fact," he added, "It looks improved."

Bernard kept his secret to himself. Why have another person's consciousness be triggered to oppose his? He thanked his doctor and left. Now, a year later, the condition has improved even further, and surgery is no longer being considered.

YOUR EYES AS A CHANNEL FOR HEALING ENERGY

In the above Action Plan, you used your hands and used your visualizing ability.

The eyes are a two-way street of psychotronic energy. However, just as we interfere mentally with the flow of psychotronic energy with negative thoughts and attitudes, we also interfere with the psychotronic functioning of our eyes.

The Environmental Health and Light Research Institute in Sarasota, Florida, headed by Dr. John Ott, is devoted to the promotion of full spectrum glass. Ordinary glass cuts out ultra-violet light. Ordinary eyeglasses, window glass, and bulb and fluorescent lighting glass cut out portions of the light spectrum. It becomes unnatural light. But now scientists realize that the body needs all of the colors that nature provides.

The American Society of Photobiology at Stanford's School of Medicine, headed by Dr. Kendrie Smith, is confirming the health benefits of the full spectrum of natural light.

One psychiatrist, Dr. H. L. Newbold, believes that the Food and

Drug Administration should look into glass products that rob our eyes of the nourishment they transmit to our body via natural light.

Apparently, the full spectrum light stimulates the optic nerve which sends out impulses to the hypothalmos. From there it travels to the pituitary gland. These two glands have a profound effect on all the other glands, that regulate the body.

Light energy and psychotronic energy are not the same, but they are closely related. Light and enlightenment.

Here is an Action Plan to harness light energy to work for your health through the psychotronic channels of the eyes. It is done on a clear sunny day.

Action plan to use solar energy for health

Sit with your back to the sun in the direct sunlight with eyes closed. Do not wear sunglasses or other glasses.

Imagine the sun pouring through your body from the top of your head on down, knowing that, as you do, all cells of your body instantly benefit.

Blink eyes open. Close immediately.

Feel the brilliance of the sun flowing through the back of your head, out through your eyes energizing all that you see, benefiting everything within the range of your vision.

End your session.

7

TAPPING A UNIVERSE OF PSYCHOTRONIC ENERGY TO MAKE PEOPLE WORK FOR YOU

In this chapter you acquire the key to turn failure into success with your psychotronic power—how to make everything go well for you, how to change from a bored follower to an enthusiastic leader. In the process, the whole world seems to work for you; the reason being, it does! To permit this to happen fully, you may need to take special note of the instructions on how to protect yourself from attack by others and how to win in highly competitive situations.

Rolling Thunder, spiritual leader for the Shoshone tribe, is describing his work in ending droughts. Witnesses say they have seen him call forth rain and thunder at will, curing disease, and healing wounds. He tells his audience how he uses his consciousness to do this. Rolling Thunder talks about the energies in the universe that work with his energy.

Sharing the speaker's platform with Rolling Thunder are Dr. Roy Menninger, Dr. Elmer Green, Dr. Carl Simonton, Rabbi Herbert Weiner and Dr. William McGarey, to name a few–focusing on biofeedback, psychotronics, spiritual mysticism, and the psychic healing work of the late Edgar Cayce.

It bodes well that mankind is now able to share these many approaches to total health–bioenergetics, mind/body interaction, altered states of consciousness, acupuncture, and psychic diagnosis, without one orthodox practitioner getting white around the lips as another practitioner contradicts all the "standard" knowledge each spent so much money learning and so many years using.

Man is growing up. He is becoming mature enough to understand his real power–psychotronic power.

There is a bird in the Galapagos Archipelago that uses a tool. This thrush does not have a beak long enough to get into the holes caused by worms in dead wood so it breaks off a twig, holds it in its beak and uses it to pry out the worms. This is one of a very few uses of a tool, other than by man, that we know about. Survival is the mother of invention.

To survive, man will now need to understand his psychotronic power because it will be the key tool in his current stage of evolution. Those who do not learn to use this tool will be at a total disadvantage. Those who learn to use it, but who misuse it will be at a partial disadvantage. Those who learn to use it with understanding and propriety will be the privileged and advantaged.

HOW TO USE YOUR PSYCHOTRONIC POWER SO AS NOT TO HURT OTHERS

The key to understanding your psychotronic power and using it in a way that will make you a privileged person lies in your acceptance of one vital fact: Your survival may not be at the expense of other human life. If you use psychotronic power to help yourself at the expense of others, you lose. If you use psychotronic power to help yourself while you help others, too, you win.

This is not moralizing, it is energy at work. Add plus energy to an equal amount of minus energy and the total is zero–no result. The reason for the totalizing is that we are really not as separate as our separate bodies seem to indicate. We are part of all consciousness, all life, all psychotronic energy.

No, it is not moralizing, but it yields the same results. What spiritual leaders have been intuitively or scripturally teaching for millennia is now being proved valid by scientists. Use your psychotronic energy to benefit others as well as yourself and you become a privileged person.

UNIVERSAL CONSCIOUSNESS–SCIENCE OR RELIGION

There is another vital fact: The path you choose for your survival is smoother when it coincides with the Universal "path" or purpose.

Uri Geller, the man who is able to bend forks and make broken watches begin to work again–all with the power of his mind, cannot always perform at will. He frequently must wait until he gets a feeling that the time is right. It is as if there is "agreement" from a larger consciousness.

Dr. Edgar Mitchell, head of the Institute of Noetic Science, and a researcher at Stanford Research Institute, says that there is now scientific evidence pointing to qualities or properties of space, such as "agreement."

It is particularly appropriate that Dr. Mitchell, eleventh man on the moon, is now exploring consciousness. Outer space will probably hold many surprises for us. But inner space is already stealing the show.

Persons able to go deep within inner space have been able to predict what we will find in outer space. These predictions have been borne out by subsequent sightings of the reverse side of the moon and by Mars probes. Maybe we will discover life on Mars, or some other planet. But we have just begun to discover the true nature of life on earth.

Scientists are discovering that you have the means to create changes in material forms by merely "willing" it so. They are finding evidence of an energy associated with consciousness that ignores time and space and accomplishes what we have thought up until now to be impossible.

It may be years before we know the whole story. Scientists in the 1960's would not even tell each other what they were discovering. When I was an undergraduate at the Massachusetts Institute of Technology in the 1930's, naively interested in frontiers of the mind, none of the faculty I talked to and only a handful of the students would admit of an interest in the mind as an area of potential exploration.

Today scientific eyes stare and scientific jaws drop in amazement at what they see in the laboratory. And they are beginning to talk about it.

It sounds as though science is coming very close to occult areas. It is indeed. And it is erasing the former noman's-land between religion and science. This is important to us at this point in the use of our psychotronic power, as you will now see.

When you attempt to influence other people you are involving other units of consciousness, which, like you, are part of Universal Consciousness.

When a healer like Rolling Thunder evokes a healing, he is getting the assistance of energy of consciousness outside his own. When a Christian prays to Jesus, help comes. When a Hawaiian kahuna calls on the ancient gods and on his aumakua (Higher Self), the call is "heard."

Consciousness is in contact with all of its parts, all of the time. To the religionist, God is always with us. To the scientist, the energy of consciousness surrounds us. To a lay person like say, Ethel Waters, "His Eye Is on the Sparrow."

To you, interested in bettering your life, you better your life when you better any life. Understand this and the cables between you and the Cosmic Psychotronic Generator become heavy duty, capable of any load you put on it.

HOW TO GET THE PEOPLE YOU WORK FOR TO WORK FOR YOU

Albert B. worked for a board of education. He helped with communications, writing a community newsletter and whatever brochures or news releases the superintendent or school principals requested. It was an easy job but it did not pay very well and Albert needed more money. So, he was really not happy with his job.

He decided to use his psychotronic power to accelerate a change for the better. He went to his relaxed, or alpha, level of mind and "saw" himself doing more than he was asked to do. He "saw" himself improving communications with form letters, flyers, and community events "beyond the call of duty."

Immediately through his contacts with the schools on necessary work, he began to get ideas for additional activities. Each time he submitted the idea for one of these activities, it was enthusiastically received. He was given the go ahead repeatedly. Community support for the school system grew. Albert began hearing that complimentary things were being said about him.

Soon he began getting calls from neighboring school superintendents. Could Albert work for them, too? There was nothing in his working arrangement which prohibited this. Within two years, Albert was working for six boards of education. He was happy, more energetic, enthusiastic. He was working a lot harder. But who wouldn't be for six times as much pay! Boards of education, school superintendents, and other educators looked to him for public relations advice.

The key here was: Albert was being led by the nose. He made the decision to change that—to himself become the leader.

If you are in a job that is limiting, you can break out of those limits—financially, creatively, socially. You may be doing more but it will feel as if you are doing less. Here is how:

Action plan to change from follower to leader

Go to your "special room."

See yourself "harnessed" in your job routine doing what you are told needs to be done.

Add something extra to the scene. See yourself doing something that you think needs to be done which will add to the productivity or efficiency. See yourself expending additional resourcefulness, time, or energy to do this on your own initiative.

Bring your immediate superior into the scene and explain the advantages. Talk with your hands. Point to visual aspects. Expect a positive, pleasant response. It comes.

Discuss the activity with colleagues and others involved. Again use your hands and emphasize visual aspects. See a similar response from them.

Repeat the "add" step above, again seeing yourself doing this extra function. See a calendar showing tomorrow's date, or the date you will start, and a clock showing the time you do it.

End your session, feeling the harness gone, and, instead, the reins in your hands.

This is an action plan that, when repeated, becomes a rung-by-rung climb up the organizational ladder. As you activate yourself to go one step beyond the required routine, and as you activate others to understand your desire to benefit the firm and therefore themselves, you become an irresistible leader. People step aside and make way for you. The usual competitive or hostile obstructionist does not materialize. Instead, people seem to root for you, even work for you.

The university scene is a competitive one. This "throws" many students not ready for competition. Even highly intelligent students fall by the academic wayside.

Trudy R. was having difficulty in college. She was getting C's and D's—averaging about 2.3. She was bored, unable to keep her mind on her teachers or studies, and especially nervous about taking examinations.

Still Trudy was a bright person. She understood people, even herself. She decided it was high time to take her own consciousness "in hand." She used several of the procedures in this book to relax and use a "special room" to program her own energy of consciousness. She "saw" herself enjoying her college work, confident in exams, and receiving higher marks.

She began to take more interest in her studies. Exams were fun. Concentration became effortless. The very next semester she got a 4.0 average without any cramming and no hard mental work.

Something happened in Trudy's *head.* But something just as important happened in Trudy's *world.* Her professors were more friendly, understanding, and helpful. They, too, changed. It was as if something bigger than both Trudy and the faculty had entered the picture.

HOW TO GET HELP FROM UNSEEN FORCES

We are born into this world. We come from somewhere. As an infant, our mind appears to be "not of this world" yet. The doctor gives us a slap and we cry. That's of this world. But, eyes closed, not reacting to outside sights, sounds, touch and smells, we sleep.

Then gradually we begin to awake. "He smiled." "She said ma-ma." "He reached for my hand."

We are becoming world oriented. Our mind is becoming aware of our five senses. We are beginning to perceive this planet, this physical world we live in, with our senses. In fact, we gradually emerge even more completely into the sense world, devoting more and more of our awareness to learning how to master the physical world. In the process, we leave behind another realm.

Actually, our mind has never left this other realm. It is just totally obsessed with survival in this sense world that appears to be all that is. Once our mind is "reminded" of the other realm from whence it came, it is able to function there, too. It is like remembering that we are not only citizens of this material world, but we are also citizens of a nonmaterial or spiritual world.

As citizens of the nonmaterial world we are able to use our minds in ways that transcend the limited sensory activities which monopolize our lives in this physical world. As citizens of the nonmaterial world we can use our minds in ways which permit us to change conditions in the physical world–effortlessly.

It would appear that within this nonmaterial world lies the blueprint for this physical world. By going to a deep (relaxed) level of mind, we contact this nonmaterial world. There, we can free ourselves of the shackles of time and space. We can go instantly to any place and be aware of what is happening there–merely by wanting to know.

We can also be at any point in time, past or future, instantly, and be aware of what is happening–merely by wanting to know. Once we know, we may want to change something. So we visualize that change taking place. Lo and behold, it happens!

In a future chapter we will go into step by step Action Plans to detect future events. Meanwhile, our present interest is in engineering consent by what you might call unseen powers to help us. These powers are in the nonphysical world. They are the powers of consciousness, and so not subservient to time and space of the physical world. Still they are energy at work–psychotronic energy.

These are the unseen powers touched by prayer, evoked by chants, and triggered by affirmation. But when you use your psychotronic energy to contact these powers, you are "talking their language."

In the next Action Plan you use your deep relaxation (alpha), your special place under the skylight, and your rapport with the universe to enlist the help of unseen powers to move other people to assist you. The more valid the purpose–and validity is measured in terms of survival and the betterment of many–the more successful you will be in this Action Plan to engineer the consent of these unseen powers.

Your sincerity is known to this universal consciousness in which unseen powers reside. "Dirty tricks" are out. It may be good public relations for you to project the image of a "good guy." However, for good cosmic relations you must *be* a "good guy."

Action plan to enlist the support of unseen powers

Go to your "special room" under the skylight.

Be aware of the vastness of the universe, the billions of stars in a galaxy, the billions of galaxies.

Feel awe, respect, yet love for the vast universe, of which you are part.

Ask permission to speak to universal consciousness that fills all space.

Wait until you feel you have received the go ahead. This could be in an instant or a minute or so.

State your problem.

Request assistance, ending ". . . if it is the will of universal consciousness."

End your session.

Some of the types of problems for which this Action Plan is appropriate are:

- Management-labor controversies where it is not a question of who is right but what is right.
- Penal or judicial situations where the need is for justice to prevail.
- Club, church, or group problems where dissidence is interfering with accomplishment.
- Personal relations between neighbors, colleagues, friends, relatives, where cooperation is needed.
- An individual relationship where the person plays a key role in your life, exerting influence over others.

Some specific examples of appropriate and inappropriate situations for this Action Plan might help to apply it properly.

Wrong: To get people to vote for you or your candidate.
Right: To get people to vote for the best candidate.
Wrong: To escape a painful decision.
Right: To induce an understanding decision.
Wrong: To force people to do your bidding.
Right: To enlist the agreement and rally the enthusiasm of people to do what is right.

If you use this Action Plan in line with the above principles, you can enlist unseen powers to help you:

- Get something for nothing
- Melt away evil influences
- Paralyze people bent on your failure
- Make new friends, ready to help you in many ways
- Win contests, votes and campaigns
- Enlist supporters to fulfill your personal goals

Stanley A. moved away from his town because the people were insular and unsocial. It was difficult to break into closed circles. However, when he arrived in his new home about twenty miles away, he found the same situation. After a year of getting nowhere in his efforts to become part of the new town's civic, political, or social activities, he realized that moving again would do no good, that he needed to change his own consciousness to effect a change.

He used relaxation and imagery to see himself competent and sharing that competence with others. Then he enlisted the aid of unseen powers in the universal consciousness, as described in the above action plan.

Within a short time the following three events took place;

1. He signed a petition at a street corner to get an independent candidate on the ballot for mayor, and was himself asked to be on the ticket for one of the elective posts.

2. He got into a conversation with a young lady sitting next to him at a lunch counter. It turned out she edited the local weekly paper as a part-time pursuit, was leaving town and would he be interested? He got the job.

3. While buying a gift for his wife's birthday, he got into a conversation with the store owner about mental health. She was just forming a clinic. He became a lay director.

Stanley did not win the election, but he did win many friends and, through his activity, as well as his editorship of the local paper and work in the area's first mental health clinic, he became a key figure in the community. It was all quite satisfying, but he knew he could not take all the credit for this overnight success himself.

He had "outside" help.

HOW TO PROTECT YOURSELF FROM UNSEEN POWERS THAT ARE OUT TO GET YOU

When Hitler pasted swastikas on photographs of buildings located on the main streets of European capitols he planned to conquer, he was not only triggering his own psychotronic powers to rally the necessary forces on his side but also creating the necessary weaknesses on the other side to accomplish his aims.

It all boomeranged on him, because it was not in the common good. But meanwhile millions of people perished. Great harm was done before the boomerang returned.

In Haiti, the voodoo arts have been used to further individual aims often without thought of what is right. The voodoo witch doctor might create a doll with his hands, see it as the victim he is out to kill, stick pins in it, and through the use of hands and eyes focus enough psychotronic energy to harm, even destroy, that person.

For many years Hawaiian kahunas, or holy men, had to operate in secrecy because they, too, were taking the law into their own hands and deciding that somebody was to die. The kahuna "death wish" has sent many of its victims to hospitals with a creeping paralysis that doctors are helpless to stem, leading to stoppage of the lungs and heart. It is said to be accomplished by enlisting the help of some newly departed soul who is too confused to know any better.

The late president of Chad, a country that stretches from the Libyan Sahara south to the thick forests of equatorial Africa, held his country in the grip of witchcraft for years. Ngarta Tombalbaye not only had his subjects undergo secret occult rites to keep them in line, but he is said to have imported witch doctors from Haiti and enlisted unseen powers in the spirit world to perpetuate his power.

Psychotronic power used against people boomerangs. There were multiple rebellions, and Tombalbaye was cut down by a burst of gunfire from his own army. Many people who have hostile intentions are unknowingly using psychotronic power for harm and enlisting unseen forces, attuned to that level of consciousness, to help them accomplish that injury and harm.

The person who is equipped to use psychotronic power for good, as prescribed in this book, needs to be aware of protective uses, too. Any hostile feelings or critical thought aimed at you is a missile. Its effect can be as minor as the cork from a popgun or as deadly as the lead of a machine gun. It depends on the psychotronic energy of the sender.

Here is how to protect yourself:

Action plan for protection against psychotronic attack

Relax wherever you happen to be when you feel in need of protection, eyes closed.

Create a plastic sphere around you.

"See" it with your eyes.

"Feel" it with your hands. It is transparent. Light energy can enter. However, it is polarized so that only positive psychotronic energy can enter. Negative thoughts bounce off and return to the sender.

Open your eyes, knowing that you are protected against psychic or psychotronic attack.

HOW TO USE PSYCHOTRONIC POWER IN COMPETITIVE SITUATIONS

Life does not often permit people to work on your side—for you or with you. You would not expect a salesman for your competitor to sell your product. Nor would you expect members of the opposing team to root for your team.

Still, there are effective ways to "psych" out the opponent. An internationally known tennis player frequently "puts on a show" of anger, humor or other emotional outbursts to win the attention of the spectators. This one-sided attention reinforces him, drains his opponent.

In October 1975, a football team that had not won a game that season played a team that had won every game it played that season. The winless Kansas City Chiefs hosted the undefeated Oakland

Raiders. For several days prior to the game, the players in the weak Chiefs developed a sense of unity on the team. Players who up until then talked only football together, socialized and fanned the flames of comraderie. They became in that short time a team in the true sense bound by friendship, mutual respect, and love.

Head coach Paul Wiggin encouraged this strong feeling of unity. Moments before the kickoff the Chiefs were dancing around jubilantly and hugging each other as if they had already won the game.

In fact, they had. No power is greater than psychotronic power. When the first quarter ended, the Chiefs held an astonishing 21–3 lead, confounding all the experts. The crowd gave the Chiefs a standing ovation, the first of many in that game when the 60,000 people jumped to their feet in wild acclaim.

Of course, that extra spectator psychotronic energy, helped the Chiefs, too. They won 42 to 10!

"I know this may sound silly," Wiggin was later quoted in the press as saying, "but love contributed to our success today."

In that game, the Raiders lost three fumbles and had three passes intercepted. The Chiefs lost no fumbles, and had only one pass interception. It was as if the heightened morale of the Chiefs sapped the morale of the Raiders.

Love, morale, enthusiasm, optimism–it all boils down to a state of consciousness. That state can be a winning state or a losing state. High psychotronic energy to win or high psychotronic energy to lose. The choice is up to the team. The Chiefs chose to win. They built up psychotronic energy with love and enthusiasm.

Teams–whether athletic or business, social or religious, educational or political–can build up their psychotronic energy to win with dramatic results.

One person on that team needs to trigger the action. It can be you. Here is how:

Action plan to ignite team psychotronic power for victory

Go to your "special room."

Call each member of the team or group into your "room" one at a time.

Speak about what you want to have happen, how a loving feeling of unity can help every member of the team.

Look each person straight in the eye as you express your admiration and repeat similar praise felt by others toward that person.

Use your hands, grasping the person by the hand, patting on the back, hugging, etc.

Call the entire team or group into your "room" and suggest a coffee rally or social. See them enthusiastic about the idea.

A day or two after completing the above Action Plan discuss such a coffee or social get together with one or two people who seem to show some positive effects from your psychotronic effort. Get them to join you in proposing and pushing for the event.

Let the event then be the "kick-off" of a new sense of teamwork and loving cooperation. Sing, affirm, cheer to build up psychotronic power to *win!*

If the group might seem receptive to a moment of silence together, take a chance and propose it. Your work in the above Action Plan may have paved the way for this to happen. If so, this is how to proceed:

Group action plan for victory

Arrange chairs in a circle.

Sit, holding hands, eyes closed, relaxed.

Feel, togetherness, oneness, mutual respect.

See the group working together. Each person visualizes the group cooperating in harmony and efficiency, being effective and successful.

End with a previously arranged affirmation—a positive statement for reaching the group's goal—vocalizing together with belief and enthusiasm!

HOW GROUPS WORK AGAINST THEMSELVES AND HOW TO REVERSE THE FAILURE PROCESS

Dr. Norman Vincent Peale brought positive thinking into the awareness of millions. Dr. Maxwell Maltz brought self-image into the awareness of more millions. Combine the two concepts and you get a powerful result: positive thinking about your limitless abilities.

If individuals were to have this resulting concept ingrained as a way of consciousness, they would be generating psychotronic energy at a rate many times normal.

In a recent published interview, Dr. Allen Fay, a New York psychiatrist on the faculty of the Mt. Sinai School of Medicine, stated that when people give themselves negative messages, such as life is a disaster and there is nothing they can do about it, they are letting go of the reins of life. When they begin to acknowledge that they are not the creature of circumstances but the creator of circumstances, they take control of their life.

Groups are guilty of the same kind of failure thoughts as individuals. But groups are even more successful at it. The reason is that psychotronic power builds up geometrically. Two negative consciousnesses generate not twice as much psychotronic failure, but four times as much. Three, nine times; four, sixteen times–the square is what governs.

Little wonder that the curve of business is watched by corporate executives on a day to day basis. A downturn signals double trouble–not only external causes, but the compounding of resulting internal causes, with the latter probably more difficult to reverse. A downturn can be reversed. Positive psychotronic energy can be harnessed to trigger a group dynamics that can turn any depressed state of conditions into a flood of prosperity.

The previous group Action Plan can be adapted to meet any adverse conditions. You, the reader, need to start the "action." Others join that action, making themselves known through their own attitude, encouraged by your psychotronic energy, and expressed by their word or action.

From then on it snowballs as more people get "turned on." It snowballs as the square of the numbers involved. What was, only a few days before, a dismal tone of despair and falure, becomes a vital exuberance that will accept nothing less than resounding success.

This is nothing new. It happens every day. It also fails to happen every day. Now its happening is not a matter of chance. It depends on you–the application of your psychotronic power. You are in control.

8

MIND OVER MONEY–TURNING PSYCHOTRONIC POWER INTO MONEY POWER

In this chapter you learn to use the alpha (relaxed) level of mind to trigger a flow of limitless money into your life. Because psychotronic energy is at work, the money can come from many different directions. You learn to focus this energy on your business and cause steady improvement without limit, to climb the organizational ladder as high as you wish to go, to form new sources of income, as many as you wish. Finally, you learn how to tap information that can enable you double or triple your wealth.

A man from New Orleans has the uncanny ability to predict stock prices, commodity trends, and profitable investments. Ron Warmoth has helped hundreds to strike it rich in gold, oil and minerals by locating rich veins and drilling areas. In California he made six oil strikes worth 50 million for one client.

The Missoula Chapter of the Montana Mining Association used these words in a written testimonial to him: "Ron Warmoth does possess an unusual and unique ability to locate veins and deposits of minerals."

This unusual and unique ability is not one that Warmoth has trained or acquired. He claims that he was born with it and that he is, therefore, a natural psychic. This means he does not have to use an Action Plan to function mentally in amazing ways. "Let me see a map of the area," he says. Then in a moment, he points with his finger. "Here." And the minerals are there.

You and I are not born psychics, at least to the extent that Warmoth is. We need to develop the ability. To do this we need a system, a method.

A Chicago couple need money. They have just learned a method to function psychically—to detect information at a distance and to make things happen for survival. Money is a survival material. They decide to apply what they have learned to win a lottery.

They relax. They see themselves in a blue framed mirror with many problems. Then they change the frame of the mirror to white and see themselves winning a large amount of money in the lottery as their ticket number is chosen.

Each does this on his or her own. They repeat it several times a day for a week prior to the drawing. They win $300,000.

The method they use is a Silva Mind Control method. But it does not matter whether you follow a prescribed commercial method or a psychotronic engineer's method. The energy of consciousness is real energy and it delivers—especially money.

THE SUBCONSCIOUS MIND—COMPUTER EXTRAORDINARY

Dr. Douglas Dean of the Newark College of Engineering studied some five hundred successful businessmen and discovered they all rated high when tested on intuitive functioning. Many admitted to ignoring statistical reports and instead acting on strong hunches. ("Don't quote me on this. My stockholders may find out.")

The energy of thought is a very real creative energy. When you get right down to it, everything that man has created has indeed existed first at his thought level, usually in the form of mental pictures held while in a problem-solving mental "posture." It leads to sketches, diagrams, blueprints, working drawings, buildings.

Color it alpha.

Now that we see the tremendous amount of information that can be stored by a computer, we are beginning to understand the mind better.

The part of the mind that is not used in moment-to-moment awareness is called the subconscious mind. The subconscious mind has three main functions which we can now identify:

1. It keeps us alive.
2. It carries out instructions.
3. It stores data.

Keeping us alive means beating our heart, operating our lungs, digesting our food, and causing all of the systems in our body to function.

Our survival is linked to health, money and job, love, human relations. Decisions regarding these matters come predominantly from the computer-like subconscious mind, even though we believe we are "thinking it over."

Past programming is what makes most decisions for us. We buy a certain kind of bread. We brush our teeth twice a day. We like a certain type of person. Past conditioning or programming can make us radiantly healthy, abundantly wealthy, and eminently successful. It is also the cause of every curse known to man.

Positive suggestions accepted while at alpha level become a part of programmed behavior instantly.

A half century ago Emil Coué had people in Europe and America look in the mirror and repeat over and over, "Every day in every way I am getting better and better." In time many had noticeable results. However, he did not know about the alpha level of mind—the relaxed level.

At alpha you get immediate results. At this level of mind, the words or mental pictures go directly into the computer banks without any critical analysis, personal self-doubt, ands, ifs, or buts.

Instruct the mind to produce money and the brain neurons in charge of conscious thought begin inductive, deductive, and associative thinking processes.

The neurons that work below the level of conscious thinking begin their processes, too. They supplement the work of the conscious thought neurons but they also are in touch with brain neurons in other people who might help to solve the problem.

Science is not sure, as of now, whether this is direct neuron communication or neuron-to universal consciousness-to neuron communication. But to the utilizer of this psychotronic energy, it does not matter, any more than it matters to the flipper of a light switch whether the energy is coming from batteries behind the wall or an area generator miles away.

WHAT HAPPENS WHEN YOU INSTRUCT THE MIND TO PRODUCE MONEY

For millennia man has been creating space in his own image. There is a God, or gods, or Son of God. There are constellations that affect man's life. And down here on earth, there are gods of the volcano, of the ocean, of the trees, and of the rain.

The concept of God can place any philosophy into a tight religious framework. Maybe for the purposes of communication it would be best for us to free ourselves from the semantics of this and from stereotypes in speech or thought. Now, so freed, we can think in terms of space as an extension of ourself.

Suppose you want to move something with your hand. To do so, you need your hand's permission. It does not withhold such permission unreasonably. But if it is broken or numb or has a valid reason, it will refuse.

Suppose space, as an arm of yourself, behaved similarly? This is a concept not too far removed from the God concept or the Edgar Mitchell continuum concept. As an arm of yourself, space would have to agree to act in your behalf. To get agreement from space you would have to "ask" or engineer that agreement in some other way.

Asking can be prayer. Engineering of consent, as Bernays defines public relations, can be picturing at the alpha level, *knowing* it to be so—a type of space relations.

There is one Oriental healer the writer knows who chants or prays to every saint that was cannonized, every angel that was ever named, every prophet that ever lived, and asks for a healing. He touches all the bases. It takes him fifteen or twenty minutes—but people are healed.

There is a clue in this to contacting space or whatever space is itself permeated with. We give this space filler names–names of deities, angels, departed spirits. Maybe this has validity. But valid or not, this space filler becomes active with a consented-to wish, a consented-to prayer, a consented-to mental image. It is as if it is an arm of our consciousness.

Are you ready to ask "space" for abundance? Then you are ready to treat space as intelligent, logical, reasonable, cooperative. This is the necessary attitude.

For the following Action Plan to be productive, you need to purify your consciousness of intellectual clutter, mundane pressures, and people problems. You need to be as pure as space itself in order to be attuned to it. This takes a Pre-Action Plan:

Pre-action plan for becoming space minded

Relax in a chair and breathe deeply.

Imagine all impurities leaving your body and consciousness with every exhalation.

Think of the space above where you are.

Go into that space instantly; imagine you can look back down at yourself sitting in the chair.

Continue this trip into space, past the coast, above the planet, past this solar system, out of the galaxy.

Feel love for this galaxy and all of the billions of galaxies "out there."

Return instantly the way you came, knowing you are in closer touch with space.

After completing this Pre-Action Plan, you are ready for the "main event," an Action Plan to win universal consent for abundance in your life.

Action plan to attract more money

Go to your "special room" and sit under the skylight.

Project your consciousness to outer space.

Talk out loud to space in a reasonable way, covering in a logical way:

The nature of your money problem
What amount of money would help you solve the problem
Exactly what you will do with the money.

Use your hands in talking and visualize the points you make in the "conversation."

Promise to give a sacrifice as a sign of your sincerity and respect.

End your session, knowing that at the moment of sacrifice, the money will be on its way to you.

Sacrifice by doing one or more of the following types of actions: Skip a meal, make a donation to a cause, feed some birds or animals.

WHY ALPHA HELPS MAKE PSYCHOTRONIC ENERGY PRODUCE BETTER FOR YOU

Why do mental images work better at the alpha level? "Why" is usually a wasteful question, but it might be of value to give this one a try. As we retreat from physical activity and from the beta world of sensory input, we get a step closer to the way we were when we were born—a step closer to our source. This source of ours is really the space filler that acts as our extension. Maybe we have always been part of our source, part of the consciousness that fills space, and still are.

This is overly simple in its conceptualization and verbalization. Actually the truth is unfathomable because it is like an infant without depth and without dimension. When Jesus was asked, "What is truth?" he stood silent. His silence spoke more than cold words.

If we call the intelligence that permeates space the Infinite, and man the finite, then what life must be all about is that the Infinite is becoming conscious of itself through the finite. Or, as somebody once said, "God became man so man could become God."

Can it be that the thousands of years of man's philosophizing that there is a spiritual (nonmaterial and intelligent) basis to the universe as expressed in theological and metaphysical literature has not been in vain? We are consciousness. Our body is a place for consciousness to particularize,* at a particularized plane we call the material world.

Our consciousness is energy, able to affect the energy we call

*I use the word particularize to mean form into smaller units or particles.

matter, because it is closely "related." Our consciousness is really part of a larger Superconsciousness, or Cosmis Consciousness, which works with us if and when we get its consent. To get this consent we need to be in "touch." To be in touch, we need to be closer to it—at alpha.

HOW TO USE PSYCHOTRONIC POWER TO IMPROVE YOUR BUSINESS

Go to alpha. Visualize. Use your hands. Can you think of applications of this procedure that will help your business.

Alfred G. owned a shoe store. It was a marginal operation. Advertising did not seem to bring in more profit than it cost. Pedestrian traffic passing his store was fairly good, but they were the people who were on their way to or from work, intent on getting there.

He decided to use a triggering device to catch the attention of passersby. Did he use a flashing light? A revolving shoe display? An animated contraption? No, he used a tiny circular piece of red paper glued to the bottom of the store window.

Then he did some psychotronic work at home nightly: He went to his relaxed alpha level, entered his "special room," visualized the store window "wearing" the red circle, seeing people's attention called to it, and, if shoes were a need, their attention then turning to the shoes.

At first there was no improvement. But he persisted for a week. Then people began to stop in front of his window. Some came in. Some of those who came in bought. Inside of another week he recorded a ten percent increase in his volume.

Sidney P. was an insurance salesman. He canvassed prospects obtained through newspaper advertisements offering free booklets. His biggest problem was getting past the front door. People always had some excuse to ask him to "come back some other time."

He, too, harnessed psychotronic energy to improve his "prospecting." Before starting out, he relaxed, went to his "special room" in his imagination. Then he saw himself being greeted at the door in a friendly way by people who needed his insurance services. He saw himself selecting the correct names and addresses for that evening's work—people who would be home and who would listen to his proposal.

Again, it took perserverance, but within a week Sidney P. began to see a difference. Nothing spectacular, but in his business, just one good contact an evening pays off. And it paid off well for him.

The difference in the approaches of the shoe retailer and the insurance salesman points up the need to adopt the application of psychotronic power in your business.

One basic procedure acts as the framework: You relax, moving into your alpha level of mind where brain waves slow down and become more synchronized with universal consciousness. Then you visualize your business activity in some constructive way. Here are some:

- A real estate agent sees "For Sale" signs change to "Sold."
- An artist sees his or her paintings radiating a light that touches people.
- A direct mail solicitor sees his own energy entering his mailing pieces and making them come "alive."
- A restaurant owner injects his food with "aliveness" and visualizes the tables filled as people are attracted to his "survival" fare.
- A taxi driver sees himself continuously in the right place at the right time for picking up fares and beating the traffic.

Calling the above "the adaptor," here is the Action Plan:

Action plan to improve your business

Relax and go to your "special room."

Visualize your business.

Use "the adaptor."

End your session, reminding yourself to repeat daily.

CLIMBING THE INCOME LADDER

George G. and I used to enjoy talking about numbers–like how, if the Indians had taken their twenty dollars when they sold Manhattan and invested it at compound interest, they might have more than Manhattan was worth today.

I did not know it then–this was some twenty years ago–but George was doing some creative daydreaming about his own life, using numbers. He figured if he continued to get raises from the plastics company he was working for at the same rate as the past few years, he would be an old man by the time he had the kind of money he felt he was worth. On the other hand, if he changed jobs every few years and got a fifty percent increase each time he did so, he would soon be in great financial shape.

I began to wonder why George was changing positions so frequently. He and his family kept moving–Pittsburgh, Cleveland, Boston. And his title became more and more impressive, like vice president in charge of sales. It was at our last meeting a couple of years ago that George told me of his job switch visions and how well they were working out. Then I told George about psychotronic energy and how he was using it in his creative daydreaming to activate his visions.

His reaction: "Nonsense–I'm just a good salesman for myself!"

There is a difference between daydreaming and creative daydreaming. Seeing yourself wallowing in the lap of luxury is idle phantasy. Seeing yourself taking specific actions leading to specific results is the application of psychotronic energy, especially if you are comfortably relaxed when you do it.

You can choose to climb the organizational ladder and attain more responsible, better paying positions in your present firm or you can decide instead, as George G. did, to climb the income ladder wherever it may lead.

Maria L. took a mind-controlling course that not only got her a good job in a school superintendent's office, but enabled her to become the personal secretary to the superintendent himself. Her images brought this about and she kept telling the superintendent about psychotronic energy and how picturing positively at the alpha level could solve some of his problems.

He just laughed this off and changed the subject. So Maria decided to use her psychotronic energy to "get to him." She "saw" him going into a conference room. She stopped him to remind him of the power of positive picturing. She "saw" him listen, then he entered the room. She also "saw" him emerge happy.

Within a few days, the superintendent told Maria to prepare the conference room. Some parents were coming. It would be a difficult morning, he predicted. "It doesn't have to be," reminded Maria. "While I get the room ready, relax and see it all working out harmoniously."

When the conference got under way behind closed doors, Maria interrupted her typing to relax and hold the same images in her mind while in her "special room." In less than an hour, everybody emerged all smiles. The superintendent gave Maria a "thumbs up" sign. "It works!" he said. Later she got a raise, and he took the course.

Norman J. aspired to be a recording artist. He had a musical group. They practiced day in and day out. Occasionally they got a club date. Then Norman learned how to tap psychotronic energy. He went to his "special room" and "talked" to an imaginary recording company. Three weeks later, the head of a recording company "happened" to hear the group at a club appearance and gave them a recording contract.

Walter N., actor, wanted a role in *South Pacific*, about to open in a resort city where he loved to stay. He used his psychotronic techniques to see himself trying out for the second lead and getting it. He did.

Millennia ago, Hermes, deified by both Egyptian and Greeks, taught secrets that were so tightly kept that the term hermetically sealed still survives. One of the secrets was a practice that made dreams come true. It went like this:

- Relax. Picture your goal accomplished. Take a deep breath and project this picture on to the air as it enters your lungs, knowing it will now enter every cell of your body.

The technique still works.

These are some of the myriads of ways that psychotronic energy works. It is activated by positive picturing at the alpha level.

All you need to do is decide on your goal, and create the mental pictures that properly reflect it.

Remember, the picture you choose should not take something away from somebody else. Psychotronic energy so directed will be opposed, not only by the individual in question whose consciousness also has energy, but by universal consciousness working for the survival of everybody.

Decide before you perform the next Action Plan just what your picture or pictures will be. They are again called "the adaptor."

Action plan for a more lucrative livelihood

Relax and go to your "special room."

Visualize your present livelihood and the life style it produces for you.

Use "the adaptor."

End your session.

Repeat once or twice a day.

CLIMBING THE ORGANIZATIONAL LADDER

If your decision is to remain in your present company and to move up in responsibility and pay, then the procedure is similar to the above except, your "adaptor" picture is in an internal organizational setting. In a way this is easier. There is more energy needed to move out and into another firm than is needed to move you up in the same firm.

However, the problem of treading on other toes becomes more of a controlling factor. Your "adaptor" image needs to be selected so as to invite the least amount of opposing psychotronic energy. Simply put: Don't step on other people as you climb.

Remember Olga Worrell's work with the cloud chamber? When disbelieving physicists viewed the experiment, nothing happened. The same is happening with similar observance of psychotronic phenomena by skeptical scientists. Things happen for scientists with expectant attitudes. If the expectation is that nothing will happen, very likely, nothing happens.

Your own expectations and belief are primary. But the resistance of another person's consciousness is also primary.

People do not need to stand in each other's way. Fear of the future, a poor self-image, and similar negative factors promote person-to-person competition where instead both would benefit by genuine person-to-person cooperation.

Do you see people standing in your way as you move up the organizational ladder? Or do you see them extending a helping hand to lift you up? The factor that makes the difference is whether your advancement promises to be a help to them or poses a threat.

Your advancement would help them if:

- Your skills benefit their performance.
- Your skills create new opportunities for them.
- Your presence adds beneficence to administration.
- Your increased responsibilities lessen their work.
- Your recognition by top management increases the chances for their recognition.

These types of changes enlist their psychotronic help. You can move ahead without their help, but you may not find your power of psychotronics anywhere near "miraculous" if theirs is in opposition to you.

The organizational chart is flexible. It can be altered to fit expediency. You do not need to see a name removed from a box in order to see your name at that step in the chart.

You can add a box:

Action plan to move up the organizational ladder

Relax in your "special room."

Invite in key people one at a time and explain why you feel the company can benefit if you are given more responsibility and a better paying post.

Explain to people you may be by-passing, also one at a time, how you are no threat to them but how your advancement can be a boon to them ultimately.

End your session knowing there has been understanding and agreement.

Prepare physically an organizational chart showing a new box in it with your name on it in the appropriate "chain of command," division, department, etc.

Post it physically on the wall. Look at it frequently. Point to your box from time to time.

HOW TO OBTAIN VALUABLE INFORMATION INTUITIVELY

We are now getting into one of the most difficult to explain aspects of human functioning. Information comes to you. It is not your information. That is, you have never learned it or experienced it, researched it or acquired it consciously. Yet, it proves to be correct information.

How did you get it? Can it be . . .

It's your inner voice?
It's your intuition?
It's your higher self?
It's the voice of the soul?
It's the voice of God?

Can you imagine any of the bespectacled scientists who are now daring to observe this in the laboratory, accepting any of these hypotheses?

In order to get "a handle" on just how we are able to pick up information by unorthodox means, it is helpful to know more about Cleve Backster, the polygraph specialist who found that plants react to people's thoughts. Backster took samples of his own blood and put them in separate containers. He put two silver electrodes into one of these containers, put the container in a shielded box, and hooked the electrode leads to an electroencephalograph. Whenever he thought of doing harm to one of the samples of blood, the other sample showed a violent reaction on the EEG.

Mary Baker Eddy would certainly nod knowingly at that. The founder of Christian Science knew the importance of positive thoughts on the well-being of the body.

But the real impact of Backster's experiment lies in the fact that cellular communication took place at a distance. Medical research explains the ability of the blood to call on various bodily resources when needed by saying such communication is handled by "chemistasis" or chemical messengers. These may exist, but there are direct communications, too, cell to cell, even over a 35-foot gap as in the Backster experiment.

Backster has also demonstrated that yogurt cells communicate over such distances. This was an automated demonstration with milk being fed to one batch of yogurt at a specific time and causing excitement on the EEG-measuring yogurt some fifty feet away.

Since Backster's work was announced, scientists all over the world have been working in this area. It is perhaps the field of research that is most demonstrative of the new discovery: the researcher is part of his own experiment. A plant reacts one way to Backster, another way to a scientist with a different attitude.

Consciousness cannot hide from consciousness. A cell's awareness, as minute as it is compared to man's awareness, is still there.

Your awareness as you read this book cannot be separated from the awareness of the cells of your body, from your family, pets or plants. Should I say something especially loving that makes you feel mellow, your whole environment is affected. The opposite is true, too.

If an order is given to the neurons of your brain, "Urgent! I need information to solve the following problem—competitors' product outselling ours; what can we do about it?" Those neurons will resonate with the information either in someone's brain miles away where that information resides or in the universal consciousness—and the answer will come.

It may come as a flash of insight.
It may come as a dream.
It may come through some "coincidence."

But come it will, because the only requirement is a sincere desire. That sincere desire is what causes the brain neurons to resonate at the necessary frequency, accurately.

There are ways to accelerate the delivery of that valuable information without waiting what might be days for the intuitive flash, dream or "coincidence."

Commercial mind courses teach the "mental screen" methodology which involves going to your mental laboratory, which is similar to your "special room" and seeing the required answer appear on an imaginary screen. This is quite effective but takes the kind of special training which these courses offer.

There is another way. It involves using symbology to induce the neurons to act within a specific time. One routine that is becoming increasingly popular is the tunnel technique:

Action plan to obtain strategic information

Imagine you are in a small boat entering a large tunnel.

Notice the pinpoint of light directly ahead; it is the other end of the tunnel.

Repeat the problem you have and know that you will have the answer by the time you reach the light.

Pretend you are drifting slowly along in the boat; feel its gentle rocking; hear the lapping waters; wait patiently for the answer.

Spend at least ten minutes on this boat ride aware of the monotony, occasionally repeating the problem, and knowing as the light at the end of the tunnel approaches your information will come.

Watch the pinpoint of light grow bigger as you approach the end of the tunnel.

End your session, emerging from the tunnel, knowing that if you do not already have the information, it is about to come.

Martin N. was a captain in the Marines and took a course in psychotronics which I gave at the Kaneohe Marine Corps Base in Hawaii. I conducted the group in this Action Plan, not because any members had expressed the need for urgent answers, but just to demonstrate the methodology.

As I completed my monotonous monologue about "the lapping of the waters and the rocking of the boat" and reminded them that "the boat is now emerging from the tunnel," Captain N. jumped up and hurried out of the room.

We did not get the answer to why the sudden exit until the next session when he explained that his unit was in a competition that required complicated logistics. He asked for insight into this problem and as the tunnel exercise ended, a unique solution had popped into his mind that required immediate implementation. It proved to be the key to his unit's exemplary showing.

Another symbology that is also successful is going into a cave several times, first seeing pictures in the wall of your early life, then pictures of your present life, then of the situation you are in that needs an answer, and finally of the answer itself.

Or you can picture yourself standing in the front of a closed curtain. The answer to your problem is on the other side. State your problem. Request the answer. See the curtain rise, creating a small opening in front of you. The opening increases in size. Finally it is large enough, and you step through—to the answer.

THE SECRET COMBINATION TO UNTOLD RICHES

This chapter started off with two Action Plans: the first, to become space minded; the second, to attract more money by getting the "agreement" of space.

That fact is significant.

It is as if there was a universal safe and there was no way to get at the real treasure unless you turned the dial in a special sequence.

Those first two Action Plans when used ahead of the subsequent Action Plans to improve your business or livelihood or get ahead on the organizational ladder, act as an "Open Sesame" to the universal store of riches.

You can storm the gates of that storehouse with physical energy alone, affirmations alone, and positive alpha picturing alone, but the results will be moderate compared to the flood that comes when you first become space minded and engineer the consent of universal consciousness.

If you belong to a religion, this does not conflict with its teachings. You can in fact adapt the words used in these two "space" Action Plans so that they conform with your religious teachings. The concept of God can be substituted for space or for universal consciousness. Also, the highest that a religion conceives–Jesus, Buddha, Mohammed–can be the intermediary in your behalf as you state your case.

The American Indians said, "The Great Spirit is everywhere."

By whatever name, universal consciousness, in which you live and have your being is all powerful–all rich. Those riches are your heritage. Activate your share.

9

PSYCHOTRONIC POWER TO OVERCOME SUPERHUMAN OBSTACLES

In this chapter you learn how to help overcome natural scourges whether ants in your kitchen or scavengers on your farm. You can control the weather, if you really must, even predict earthquakes and natural disasters in plenty of time to take life-saving steps. Finally, you learn ways to solve seemingly super-human problems quickly and easily.

What happens when an irresistible force meets an immovable body? That question has been puzzled by physicists and philosophers for decades. Now the answer is known. The winner: The irresistible force.

The reason is that the only known irresistible force is that of psychotronic power. And when psychotronic power meets an immovable body, it dissolves it.

The energy of consciousness has now been observed under laboratory conditions to dematerialize and rematerialize.

One day we will realize we have all been wizards from the start.

Scientists are busy looking for the kinds of change in the parameters of present laws that will embrace a whole new set of data. This data includes moving objects with consciousness, causing both levitation and an increase in weight with consciousness, changing the molecular structure of material with consciousness.

Consciousness–the very factor that devised these scientific laws–must now change them in order to make room for itself.

Meanwhile, realizing his newly "accepted" powers, man can move ahead using them in a controlled manner to overcome obstacles and improve his life.

OVERCOMING NATURAL SCOURGES

A group of people that meet with the author in Hawaii periodically to work on human problems–both the individual and collective kind–heard about a plague of blackbirds that hit a Maryland area. The local farmers were losing their crops. The millions of scavengers were stripping the area.

Local authorities had tried shooting off shotguns, even cannons. Now they had been there nearly two weeks and there was talk of using strong poisons.

We decided to act–five thousand miles away. We went to our "special rooms," invited the bird leaders to enter, and discussed the problem. Since each person did this in his own way, I can only describe how *I* conducted this "interview."

Staring them in the eye and pointing at them, I said, "You are hurting a lot of people. You cannot blame them for striking back. They will hurt you. Why not leave now and find some other place where you will not be causing a problem?"

That was the gist of it.

We read in the afternoon papers the next day that at six a.m. the birds had left. That was midnight Hawaiian time, one hour after the collective psychotronic power of some twenty people had been leveled at them.

Farmers are not the only people who are threatened by natural pests, insects, and scourges. Suburban dwellers can lose their peace of mind to ants, weevils, termites and cockroaches.

Poison sprays are often more dangerous to the user than to the sprayed. Psychotronic energy is far safer. You can take action against these natural invaders. However, your action needs to be on a high level of respect for life.

The late Albert Schweitzer gave up a successful professional career as an instructor in theology in Strasbourg, in the early 1900's, to study medicine so that he could be of direct service to mankind. He left Europe for remote Africa where he set up a health care center African style where Africans could receive modern medical benefits without leaving familiar surroundings. He did not impose his way, or modern man's way, on them. That could have created other problems for them. He displayed a reverence for all life styles and indeed for all life.

Dr. Schweitzer knew something. So did a man named Boone who wrote *"Kinship With All Life,"* whom I mentioned in Chapter 5. And so do the American Indians, as demonstrated by medicine men like Rolling Thunder and Soloho.

What they all were aware of is the common denominator of life that permeates it from the ant to man. The Indian calls it the Great Spirit. Philosophers call it God. Scientists now call it "a field of consciousness."

Whatever you call it, matters little. What matters is your own relationship to this common denominator.

If you feel separate, you create a separation, and psychotronic energy cannot flow across that separation. It is like the circuit is not closed unless you see it closed.

Feel this common denominator; accept it; attune yourself to all life. If you can, you are able to produce a psychotronic power that knows no limit, except the limit of "common good."

This does not mean you have to feel a brother-sister relationship with a cockroach. But you have to cancel out disgust, fear, and the urge to kill it. Instead, you have to recognize it as a living expression of some common denominator to all life which you share with the cockroach. Little wonder that people cannot get rid of ants, termites, and cockroaches.

Here is an Action Plan that helps to overcome this natural barrier and permit psychotronic energy to succeed where sprays and poisons fail.

Action plan number one to get rid of insects

Go to your "special room."

Deepen your relaxation by taking several deep breaths, each time you exhale, feel yourself getting sleepier.

Imagine that you are dreaming and the chief of the ants or other bothersome scourge appears before you, greatly enlarged, in costume, and able to speak.

Tell about your problems. Make a bargain, perhaps like, "I won't harm you and your friends if you leave within 24 hours." Assure the insect that there are other places to go that will not cause a problem such as here. Point. Stare. Gesticulate with your hands.

End your session.

Add a real life conversation when you next see such an insect where it is not supposed to be. Remind the insect of your bargain, speaking out loud, pointing at and looking at the insect. Know that the agreement will be kept. Expect it. Take it for granted.

Laura S. had ants in her kitchen. They were the very small variety that she could hardly see. They could hide in small cracks and behind tiles or baseboards and escape her spraying. If a package of food was left on the counter it would soon be attacked. Jars and other covered containers had to be constantly checked for tightness or else the pigmy ants would be into them.

Laura attended a psychotronic meeting where this subject was discussed and the results that some had with the above Action Plan shared. She decided to try it.

She was able to talk quite logically and reasonably with the "ant leader." Later, she repeated the conversation aloud to the first ant she saw on her kitchen counter. "It stopped crawling as if it was listening to me," she recounted later. Within a day the ants were no longer to be seen.

The insect kingdom keeps its "agreement." But generations come and go, often in a matter of days, and new "agreements" need to be made. Also, other types and species explore and move in. So Action Plan Number One may have to be repeated frequently.

ACTION PLAN NUMBER TWO TO GET RID OF INSECTS

When therapists began to experiment with the beneficial effects of certain colored lights on the human body, they discovered an interesting fact: A person does not have to sit under the blue light or green light for an hour, instead a photograph of that person when placed under the light will cause the same improvement.

Now a crop-spraying-by-air company has discovered that by taking an aerial photograph of a cornfield or other crop where there is an insect infestation, treating that photograph with the spray removes the insects just as effectively as spraying the crop directly.

Science cannot yet explain this. It is as if the picture identifies the spot because there is no place exactly like it anywhere, just as a photograph of a person identifies that person. Once identified, perhaps the cause-effect relationship takes place in the universal consciousness–blueprint for all that is.

If you have an insect problem and are loathe to use sprays and other poisonous substances profusely, especially around food storage and preparation areas, then this Action Plan Number Two can be used to supplement Action Plan Number One.

Action plan number two to get rid of insects

Photograph the area.

Spray the photograph with insect repellent.

Go to your "special room."

Hold the photograph at eye level, looking at it.

Close your eyes.

See the photograph become alive. It is the place itself. The insects are reacting to the chemical. The job is done.

End your session.

Farmers should experiment with this Action Plan Number Two on small local areas first before tackling more extensive pest problems.

There are many household applications. Wanda B. had a problem with fruit flies in her kitchen. She visualized a gas in the kitchen that was neutral to everything but poisonous to fruit flies. After doing the first Action Plan once she noticed the fruit flies diminished in number. After the third time they were gone.

DEALING WITH WEATHER PROBLEMS

The witnessed story is told of how Rolling Thunder once created a tornado to right a wrong.

A young Shoshone had been sentenced to a five year term in Leavenworth Prison for refusing to go to Vietnam. Since the United States treaty with the Shoshone Indians guarantees that there will be no military drafting, Rolling Thunder resolved to get the boy out of prison.

He got to the prison, accompanied by a white man friend, and demanded the release of the Indian youth. They were told that he had been transferred. That night, in a nearby motel, Rolling Thunder awakened his friend and said that the prison officials were lying. He could use fear as a weapon to release the youth. They must set out immediately.

They headed toward the prison. Rolling Thunder stopped and built a bonfire. He put certain things into it. A black funnel cloud formed over the fire. It grew in size. As they reached the prison about dawn the cloud had grown in size and lightning was crackling.

Rolling Thunder demanded that the guards deliver the youth. The tornado would rip the prison apart if they did not, he warned. The guards summoned some officers. When the tornado was nearly on top of the prison and had already ripped off a gate, they rushed inside, got the youth, brought him out, released him to Rolling Thunder and they left.

Man once thought there was no way to control pain. Now he knows there is. Man once thought there was no way to determine information other than through the senses. Now he can see it being done by those who know how.

Man still thinks that the weather is a super-human force out of his control. Except the American Indian—and the psychotronic engineer.

When a storm was approaching Honolulu, the author worked psychotronically with a number of colleagues to divert it. The storm skirted Honolulu, blowing roofs off in Kailua less than twenty miles away.

Flushed with this victory, at the next meeting, several had weather problems that they asked the group to work on.

1. A teacher was taking her class to Sea Life Park. They would arrive the next morning (Friday), about 10 a.m. "No rain, please."
2. On Saturday, a fellow was going on a hike. "Nice weather, please."
3. A woman's daughter was getting married that Sunday. There would be an outdoor reception at their Diamond Head home. "A clear day, please."

We went to work on these problems that night in our collective "special rooms."

I woke up the next morning and the sky was black. Lightning flashed every few seconds and the thunder pealed—very unusual for Hawaii. At 10 a.m. sharp, lightning hit my building and the electricity went out.

I said to myself, "OK. I promise. No more interference with the weather."

When the teacher returned from her Sea Life Park on time, she reported heavy rains going and coming, but "barely a drizzle" out there. As to the hike and the wedding, Saturday and Sunday were fine. We are not planning to work again on the weather, at least at this time.

The fact that psychotronic energy can be directed at the weather with positive results makes it a possible course of applied action. Whether or not you wish to use your psychotronic energy for this purpose is a personal decision.

Personally, if it were a question of survival, I would not hesitate to use mine again to affect the weather. But I would not again use it for convenience purposes. Somehow I think Rolling Thunder and other Indian medicine men would agree with me. So they have their rain chants.

Psychotronics is a new science and so we have to set up guidelines for its ethical, proper, and safe use. Man may not have reached a level of wisdom whereby he can produce these guidelines unilaterally—that is, on his own. He may need universal help. He may need to use trial and error, suffering the consequences of abuse and misuse until the right path is clear.

DEALING WITH EARTHQUAKES, VOLCANIC ERUPTIONS AND HOLOCAUSTS

Recently, when a large earthquake hit China, the population was warned of serious aftershocks and additional loss of life was minimized when these occurred. These warnings of aftershocks were partly derived from past experience and partly the result of information from seismic equipment. There was a third contributing information channel: animals in the zoo.

The consciousness of animals may not have the ability to think logically as does the consciousness of man. However, it does appear to be more closely attuned to intuition–the messages of nature. Animals appear to sense natural disasters and holocausts. Their survival instincts hear more clearly than ours when nature talks. Ours hears more clearly than theirs when civilization talks.

Psychotronics does not yet claim to be able to quiet earthquakes, put the cap on volcanic eruptions, or halt tidal waves. However, it can restore attunement to the messages of nature. Such attunement can help you to take evasive action or to avoid being in the wrong place at the wrong time.

There is no single Action Plan that can produce this attunement. However, every one of the Action Plans on these pages contributes to this attunement. The aspects of these Action Plans that bear most sensitively on this attunement are:

- Going to your "special room."
- Being under the "skylight."
- Being aware of the Cosmic Psychotronic Generator.
- Feeling love and respect for all plants, animals and people.
- Sensing you are part of a universal consciousness.

If you have been doing Action Plans that entail these aspects, you are then in greater attunement. You can trust your intuition, your "gut feelings."

Once you get feelings of uneasiness about where you are, a sense of nervousness about impending events, you can use the following Action Plan to get verification and possibly further details:

Action plan to check for possible impending holocaust

Go to your "special room," under the skylight.

Create a screen in the space ahead of you.

Ask for a "sign" of any impending disaster to appear on your screen.

Place a calendar and a clock near the screen.

If an image of an event appears on your screen check the clock and calendar to time it.

End your session and take whatever action comes to mind first—it is usually the most dependable.

Persons chronically afraid or others who tend toward feelings of doomsday are providing "static" due to emotional or other conditioned causes. This "static" will interfere with effective use of this Action Plan.

PSYCHOTRONIC POWER AND PRAYER POWER

A woman kneels in prayer. A child is seriously ill. She beseeches the Almighty to heal her child.

A man is tossing at sea on a life raft. He has been drifting for ten days. He prays for rescue.

A little girl prays for a doll at Christmas.

The mother's child is healed. The man at sea is rescued. The little girl gets her doll.

All coincidences? Or, are prayers answered? The religionist would say, "God has heard all three prayers and answered them." The psychotronic engineer would say that all three people have succeeded in eliciting the "agreement" of the cosmos.

A woman became interested in a geodetic dome. She wished she could have a miniature one or an easy way to make one. She was driving in town one day. As a car up ahead started when the light turned green, a package dropped out of its partly opened rear trunk. She blew the horn, but the car kept on going. She got out of her car, picked up the package. Later, when she arrived home, she opened the package. It was a geodetic dome, with no clue as to who the owner was.

A New York man needed a rare book. He heard there was a chance he might find it in Canada. He made preparations to go. Crossing Madison Avenue one day, deep in thought, he bumped into a man carrying books. They spilled into the middle of the street. He helped the man pick them up. There was the rare book he had been seeking.

Are these coincidences, prayers answered, or the energy of consciousness at work. The author is compelled to rule out coincidence. The incidence of coincidence—if that is indeed what it is—is so high as to render the word invalid or change its meaning. The author is also compelled to see no difference in "prayers answered" and "the energy of consciousness at work."

The work that Dr. Edgar Mitchell has been doing both as head of the Institute of Noetic Sciences and as a researcher for Stanford

Research Institute leads him and his colleagues to believe that science must go to a cosmology that leans much closer to religion than to classical science; that scientists are hypothesizing that perhaps there is a "fundamental ultimate consciousness that indeed governs, directs and guides the universe."

He compares this ultimate consciousness to a universal field of consciousness that permeates all space and has such properties as intention, awareness, and agreement. He sees a possibility that just as plasma can trap magnetic lines of force, changes in this field of consciousness can change and influence matter.

Compare this to the point of view of another kind of doctor—a doctor of divinity—Dr. Margaret Breece Whiting, who said, "God sleeps in the minerals, awakes in plants, walks in the animals, and thinks in man."

Yes, the no-man's-land between science and religion is now approaching every-man's-land.

The words we use matter little compared to the thoughts that we think behind those words.

The English word "shaman," meaning medicine man or priest of shamanism, has its roots in the Sanscrit word "sramanas" (meaning ascetic) and similar sounding words in Russian, German and other languages.

The religious practice of shamanism involves the summoning of good and evil spirits, the priest acting as go-between. Ji San Lee is a Korean shaman who occasionally visits the United States to demonstrate his talents through the medium of the dance. He claims to be the first shaman to cross the Pacific from Korea. Why the dance? It is the ritual by which the gods are contacted, he replies, and he goes on to explain how he conquers space through the dance and becomes infused with God.

Using shamanism as a bridge, we can see consciousness at work in all religious observances, evoking the "agreement" of universal consciousness to affect matter.

A priest on the east coast, Father G., combines his church activities with teaching a nationally popular mind course. He tells the story of how he commissioned an artist to paint a large ceiling "mural" depicting a religious scene. It was decided that it would be done on large squares of canvas and later installed on the ceiling.

When it was completed and installation began, no adhesive would hold the canvas squares to the ceiling. One might stay up a minute or two. Then down it would come.

Father G. got up there himself to supervise—to no avail. Then he decided climbing a ladder was not necessarily getting closer to God. He went to his study, relaxed and asked for a solution to appear. He "saw" a can of plain Elmer's glue standing beside a standard table iron.

In a few minutes, as unlikely as they sounded, both items were obtained and he was back on top of the ladder. The glue was applied; the canvas held to the ceiling; the hot iron was applied. There was a sizzling sound. He took his hands away. The canvas held. And has remained up.

Psychotronic energy or Divine energy?

Become like a child and you enter the Kingdom of Heaven. A child is on low brain wave frequency a greater percentage of the time. A child daydreams. A child respects his imagination.

Jesus said that if you desire something with all your heart, soul, and mind, you can move mountains. Add "expecting" to "desire" and you have "faith."

If you consider that religion is a field of inquiry toward finding a dimension at which we can communicate with universal consciousness–let us call that God–then psychotronics should be of especial interest to religious people. It so happens that hundreds of people in the ministry have taken mind courses that lead to controlled use of the energy of consciousness.

Jesus was aware of natural psychic ability: "Behold, I send you prophets, and wise men, and scribes . . ."

Paraphrasing Luke 12:2,3, "There is nothing concealed that will not be disclosed, nothing hidden that will not be made known. For what is said in darkness will be said in the light; and what is whispered in the inner chambers will be preached on the house tops."

Is this saying that there is indeed a universal consciousness?

Some new age religions call God "Infinite Intelligence." If intelligence is God, then our intelligence is an expression of our divine nature. And the more we use our psychotronic power, the more God-like we become.

HOW TO GIVE MORE SPIRITUAL DIMENSION TO PSYCHOTRONIC ENERGY TO SOLVE SUPER-HUMAN PROBLEMS

As you realize the true nature of your consciousness, you tend to use it in more idealistic ways.

Galil Gibran, author of *The Prophet* advised us not to invite a rich man to our house for dinner as he would only pay us back by inviting us to his house for dinner. Invite a poor man, he said, who cannot return the favor. Then the universe must pay you back.

The universal consciousness does indeed respond. Psychotronic work is accomplished as if by miraculous coincidence. The right people turn up at the right time. Our will is done.

However, sometimes our will is in direct opposition to "universal will." Then we wonder why psychotronic energy we put out does not work.

The process of aligning our will to the universal will is sometimes called meditation. Meditation comes in many methods and forms. Whatever methodology is used, it is aimed at relaxing the body and the mind and attuning to the universal consciousness.

It is as if you are saying, "Hey, Dad, remember me–I'm your child."

Then you really have something going for you. People who spend a few minutes a day begin to function in a way that surprises nobody more than it does themselves. Everything seems to go well–a lot better, at least, than it did before.

Psychotronic Action Plans are, to a degree, meditations–guided meditations. Increase that degree and you increase the scope of the kind of problems that respond to your one or two minutes in your "special place."

Here is an Action Plan to help solve some superhuman problem which needs superhuman help. These could be problems having to do with:

- Taking a long trip.
- Obtaining a seldom-given governmental permission.
- Getting a sizeable acquisition.
- Escaping from an impossible situation.
- Recovering from a so-called terminal disease.
- Ending an intolerable condition.

Before beginning this Action Plan it is advisable to purify your consciousness so that it is free of "static" and better able to communicate with universal consciousness. For twenty-four hours prior to the start of this Action Plan do some or all of the following purifications:

1. Fast, skipping all meals and taking only water and fruit juice.

2. Visit a church or synagogue, and spend at least fifteen minutes in quiet contemplation.
3. Avoid smoking and drinking intoxicants, or stimulants such as coffee or tea.
4. Stay out of the presence of negative, angry, or unpleasant people.
5. Avoid crowds.

With a consciousness that is elevated in vibration due to these purifying steps, you are ready to begin:

Action plan to enlist superhuman assistance

Go to your "special room."

Relax into a state of ecstatic tranquility.

Turn your awareness to space in increasing increments: the space in your room, your house, your town, your state, your country, the continent, the planet, the solar system, the galaxy, other galaxies.

Call on the universe to "hear" your problem. You may mention names of the deity, lesser deities, saints, ascended masters, any names in your culture or religion that are "step-up transformers" to the highest. But do not personify space.

Speak aloud, using your hands in prayer or supplication, requesting a solution to the problem. (Do not decide the details of this solution yourself, merely request the end of the problem).

Sit quietly for five minutes in silence and respect.

Return your awareness by the same route–galaxy, planetary system, earth, etc. to your room.

Bow your head three times, giving a psychotronic receipt or acknowledgement of the contact with universal consciousness, your thanks, and your acceptance.

UNITING PSYCHOTRONIC POWERS FROM MANY SOURCES TO DISSOLVE YOUR PROBLEM

William and Frances G. were driving in the early morning hours through a deserted countryside when their car motor suddenly sputtered and went dead.

William got out, tinkered with the carburetor and ignition system, got back in, and tried the starter. The motor started. They were on their way again. But in another minute or two the car stalled again. He got it started again but in less than a mile it stalled again. This happened again and again.

After a dozen stops and starts, when it became apparent that they would be all night getting home, Frances suggested to William that they go to their meditative level and call on higher consciousness to solve the problem. With typical masculine assertiveness, William replied, "No, I think I know what is wrong. I'll get it this time."

But he didn't. So, when the car stalled again, Frances decided to take the matter in her own hands and turn it over to "higher" hands. She sat in the car and performed the equivalent of the Action Plan above to enlist superhuman assistance. When William had done his tinkering again, he got back in the car once again and started up. This time the car purred peacefully all the way home. But the conversation inside the car was something less than peaceful as Frances tried to convince William that she had successfully summoned help from above and William tried to convince Frances that he had finally discovered "the right thing to do."

The truth is they were both right.

When superhuman help is enlisted to solve a problem, it often manifests in very human ways:

- You get an idea.
- You do the right thing.
- You receive help from another person.
- You enjoy the benefit of a happy coincidence.

Because of the everyday character of the problem-solving process, we are inclined to say "I did it." It comes through our consciousness just like any other idea we get, so we say "I got the idea to . . ."

This has a detrimental effect on the full working of psychotronic power. What it is really saying is "I don't need the rest of universal consciousness of which I am part. The part that I am is sufficient to me and my problems."

This self-credit cuts us off from the Cosmic Psychotronic Generator. We lose our connection to a vast source of miracle-making energy.

We need to do just the opposite. We need to give universal consciousness the credit for all our solutions. This seals the connection—

insures our power. This leads to what you might call the Basic Law of Psychotronic Power:

Never accept the credit for any psychotronic effects. Assign such credit mentally to a larger consciousness.

Scientists and engineers begin to shy away at such concepts. But their colleagues in advanced research continually see evidence of this larger consciousness at work.

Your neurological system, including your brain, seems to act as a sensing device not only for your conscious perception of sensory stimuli but also for information from space.

If you know the name of the book you want in the library, your consciousness can locate it. But if you know more generally the type of information you want, then the librarian must identify the book you need. It seems to be this way also in the retrieval of information or assistance from universal consciousness.

Our consciousness reaches for the help. But instead of our mind latching on to it, outside intelligence–the "librarian"–hands it to our mind. So what the Basic Law of Psychotronic Power is really saying is–don't fire the librarian.

Accept the cash, or benefits, or psychotronic power, and let the credit go to the higher sources. It keeps your contact with the Cosmic Psychotronic Generator alive and well.

If you understand the principle at work here, you can then understand why I am going to make an unusual request:

Create a special Action Plan on your own to acknowledge universal consciousness. If I do it for you, it does not "ring true." It needs to be your consciousness all the way, in order that universal consciousness zeros in its miracles on you–all the way.

Action plan to cement universal consciousness relations

(You create according to your own feelings, desires, and intentions).

You have cemented relations with the strongest possible ally. *You* are not superhuman. But you can conquer superhuman obstacles.

10

HOW YOUR HANDS CRACKLE WITH CREATIVE ENERGY TO MAKE OTHER PEOPLE'S WISHES COME TRUE

In this chapter you learn how to focus psychotronic energy with your fingers to be like a genie for anyone you wish to help and how each time it focuses higher voltage for greater "miracles" for yourself. You learn finger pointing techniques, for laser-like power. You learn to receive valuable information through your hands via a pendulum and via a finger technique, and how to put a glass of water to work with your finger energy to solve any problem.

A physicist who teaches in a university department of nuclear engineering spoke to a group of teachers of ESP and psychic functioning.

> There is a division in the society between those oriented to the physical world and those oriented to the psychic world. I am of both worlds.
>
> I have done research in physics all of my life. I am now interested in continuing that research in other dimensions. Once, a gentleman named Einstein spoke of the fourth dimension and proved this was a useful concept. I feel that this psychic realm is for real. I feel that these other dimensions–of understanding, of love–are just as real as the three we deal with in our mathematical models we call engineering and science. I would like to understand the psychic dimensions just as well as I understand these physical dimensions.

He is not alone.

He said this at about the time that other scientists were using the term "psychotronics" to designate the kind of energy that is at work in psychic functioning.

The greatest advantage of this to people in general is that they can go about using this energy to create a better life without being crucified, burned at the stake as a witch, or subjected to harrassment, ridicule and other modern means of persecution.

This use bears the promise of perfect health, immense power, unlimited wealth, and winning your heart's desire. But it does not come totally without an effort.

You do have to lift a finger.

The hands of man are one of the most highly evolved organs of his body. With some 25 joints, they are capable of 58 different motions. They are creators of comforts, crafts, cultures, civilizations, and even conversation and other forms of communication.

The Maharishi Mahesh Yogi, founder of Transcendatal Meditation, once handed the author a flower after holding it momentarily in his hands. The flower remained perfect for nearly two weeks.

If you think I am suggesting that the Maharishi invested that flower with a special energy that kept it from wilting all those days, you are perfectly right. Except that you do not have to be a guru to have this energy in your hands. You have it right now, whoever you are.

In this chapter you will learn how to use your hands in practical ways to help yourself and others to gain special benefits. More than putting life into a flower, you will make the fondest wishes of your friends and of yourself come alive.

THE LAW OF PSYCHOTRONICS

Action Plans from this chapter on will provide instructions on applying psychotronic power in special ways. These Action Plans will work even if you have not done the previous Action Plans having to do with going to your "special room" and also with hooking up to the Cosmic Psychotronic Generator and getting "agreement" from universal consciousness.

But they will work much more effectively if you have performed these previous Action Plans. You will have magnified the power of your psychotronic energy many fold.

There are other ways to magnify your psychotronic energy. Pyramid power is psychotronic power. The power of the pyramid shape, even simple living room models now available to sit under and meditate, can produce sizeable psychotronic increase in a matter of minutes. Pyramid power was originally discovered through the realization that carcasses of dead cats and dogs found in Egyptian pyramids were not decaying.

Sleeping with the head to the north is also said to increase psychotronic energy by utilizing the earth's magnetic field.

However, these ways involve the use of aids outside the sphere of consciousness. Your consciousness, properly directed, can provide you with all the psychotronic energy you can possibly use, with plenty left over.

Connected to the Cosmic Psychotronic Generator, and with the "agreement" of universal consciousness–as spelled out in previous Action Plans–you are like a powerhouse ready to electrify the world you live in.

Your hands can "crackle" with this power.

Couple your hands with your imaging faculty and you can send sizzling energy to get things done.

Other people jump to your aid. "Lucky" events take place in rapid succession. Obstacles and opponents fade. You get what you want.

Here is the Law of Psychotronics: *Do for other people first. Then do for yourself.*

In doing things for other people, you build up a credit balance in universal consciousness. When you are ready to benefit yourself, the prizes you seek have a downhill road to follow. They come much more quickly and with far less effort.

Ralph A. wanted more free time. His job as a newspaper man was far too demanding. He liked the work but he also liked traveling, playing bridge, going to sporting events and sunning at the beach.

Knowing how to use his psychotronic powers he visualized himself in all of these pursuits. But it did not happen. I advised Ralph to help other people first. Young people came to him frequently with dreams of becoming newspaper men. He had turned them away saying it was an overcrowded field. Now he decided to help them in that direction. He assisted with their resumes; told them whom to see and where; and how to act at the interview.

One day he was called in by his editor and told he was being given a new assignment: to write a column. It meant more money, more free time. It was exactly what he wanted. And, by "coincidence" the person he was to train to take over his old job was one of the young people he had recently helped.

TRIGGERING ACTION IN OTHER PEOPLE WITH YOUR HANDS

Point at another person. Now point in the direction you want him to go. Finally, "sketch" with your pointed finger on the palm of your other hand what you want him to do when he gets there.

You have just increased the desire of that person. His motivation will now be nearly irrepressible.

People have been talking with their hands even before language was discovered. When language came into use, the hands continued to be used to talk with to add emphasis (energy) to the words.

The angry taxicab driver gesticulates with his hands as he swears. The construction foreman signals with his hands as he calls for the crane. The housewife demonstrates with her hands as she explains to a neighbor what happened.

In psychotronics there are special ways to use your hands that focus your energy like a laser. One way is to point. Begin using finger pointing to help another person. There are many ways to help another person, and to point in the process:

- Point out a direction
- Point to the right person to see
- Point to the article sought.

Contrary to the taxicab driver, foreman, or housewife, you are calm as you point. Being relaxed and serene permits your energy to flow.

Take action for yourself by taking action for somebody else first—with this Action Plan:

Action plan to increase your hand energy for doing good

Give advice or instructions to somebody who has indicated his need for your help.

Point at that person, not threateningly, but softly and deftly, with the index finger of your stronger hand.

Use your hand to help you explain what the person needs to do.

Help the person get started, using your hands wherever possible.

Shake hands when parting, placing your left hand on top of his hand, thereby using both of your hands to grasp his.

Later, whenever you think of your friend's project, "see" him successful while you relax. (Going to your "special room" optional.)

HOW TO STEP UP THE POWER IN YOUR HANDS

These hand motions, gestures and movements seem simple enough. You have used them before and no miracles took place. Why now?

Well, something new has been added. You are now aware of the power in your hands. You are consciously using the hands for power. This conscious awareness converts the normal energy flow into a bolt of crackling power.

American Indians who know how can create a surge of power in their hands that make the person they touch jump back with the shock of it. Hawaiian kahunas can produce this energy in the form of heat and make their hands stinging hot. Both cultures also use a rubbing of the hands process to generate greater power in their hands.

Naturally, this is not just a mechanical process of rubbing two hands together. It needs to be done in a relaxed state, supported by the conscious awareness of exactly what you are doing.

The next Action Plan can be used once as a practice plan before being put to work for your benefit or the benefit of your friends, colleagues or relatives. In applying it in practice it is helpful to use a simple thermometer in your hand to test the temperature before and after. Hold the bulb between your finger tips for two minutes before and two minutes after. Compare the readings.

Important: Do not let the thermometer occupy your attention. If raising the temperature on the thermometer becomes your conscious concern you are turning off your psychotronic energy. The thermometer is just incidental to the procedure—a means of giving you confidence in being able to increase the power of your hands to make things happen. Saying "do not think of the thermometer," is like asking yourself not to think of a red elephant. The mind seems to move right in. So the trick is to play with the thermometer between your fingers on a few occasions to acquaint yourself with the feeling so that later you are accustomed to it and can ignore it.

How to add more voltage to your hands for greater power

Hold your hands in prayer position.

Rub the palms slowly and gently together.

"See" the Cosmic Psychotronic Generator providing you with power that enters your body at the crown of your head and flows through your arms into your hands.

Visualize the color orange surrounding your hands as you rub them slowly together.

Separate your palms keeping the tips of your fingers together, seeing the orange light getting brighter where your fingertips meet.

End by rubbing the hands vigorously together for 30 seconds seeing the orange light get brighter and brighter until it turns to white hot.

Use your hands as soon as possible in encouraging action by another person, through pointing and gesticulating.

If you are using your hands for healing purposes this Action Plan will increase their effectiveness.

If you use your hands to point to goal charts or sales curves and quotas as you project visually for attainment, your prior use of this Action Plan will increase their effectiveness.

Person-to-person relationships will be more under your control. Again, begin by doing for others before doing for yourself.

TOOLS THAT MAKE THE HANDS ACT AS IF THEY HAD A SUPER-MIND OF THEIR OWN

Dr. Christopher Hills of London owned an art gallery in Kingston, Jamaica. He had always been interested in the ability of the mind to detect information as well as project it. In fact, his home in London had become a center for consciousness growth through yoga, meditation, and other disciplines.

One evening while meditating on the beach in Jamaica he was intensely aware of the cosmos. It seemed that it was manifesting to him in more intimate terms. It was an exciting experience. Were his yoga and meditation making very real changes in his attunement with universal consciousness?

It appears that the answer was yes, because Dr. Hills began to feel energy with his hands in surges of greater awareness. He could sense north by stretching his arms out and slowly rotating until he felt the magnetic flow. He could use a dowsing rod and a pendulum to detect fine energies that were modulated with intelligence much the way radio waves are modulated with sounds of voices or music.

Dr. Hills spent time in India where this level of consciousness had been developed by gurus. He was quickly accepted by them and given the title of Maharishi, meaning great researcher, and Acharya, meaning inspired teacher.

In 1973 Dr. Hills moved to California where he founded the University of the Trees in Boulder Creek to be both researcher and teacher, emphasizing what he calls the science of Supersensonics.

In a sense this science might be called the actualizing of psychotronic power. One thing that makes it different than other sciences is that the *researcher becomes part of the research.* The experimenter becomes part of the experiment.

A mathematician comes home at night and his life is pretty much as it was. A chemist gets up in the morning and goes to work and he could be a lawyer or an accountant as far as how he feels and behaves is concerned. But the psychotronics practitioner becomes a super-man. He is able to do things that make other people gasp.

Dowsers have been using forked sticks for generations to locate water and the right spot to dig for wells. They heard it could be done so they went ahead and did it.

Today there is an American Society of Dowsers that meets once a year, usually in New England. Some can dowse for water without the help of a stick or rod. Others can dowse for minerals and other materials.

There are many theories shared on how this detection of information is able to take place. Dr. Z. V. Harvalik, a working physicist and successful dowser, calls the cause an electromagnetic stimulus received in the venal gland, forwarded to the brain and then transmitted to the muscles of the forearm.

Scientists have observed an interesting application of the detection of information with the hands. Blind people can see with their hands. Colored paper and geometric shapes can be accurately described by blind people holding their hands above the cutouts.

Falling into old patterns with their thinking, some of these scientists are calling this dermo-optic sensitivity, and hypothesizing that the cells of the skin possess miniature eyes. To the psychotronic scientist this sounds ludicrous. But to the conventional scientist who uses this approach, the psychotronic theory appears ludicrous.

While the scientists research, hypothesize, and debate, the rest of us can use whatever it is to our advantage. We can sensitize our detection of information through our hands with devices such as the divining, or dowsing, rod and the pendulum.

HOW TO GET ANSWERS THROUGH YOUR HANDS WITH A PENDULUM

Some years ago a group of fishermen were overdue in the New Hebrides area. Their families were concerned. An air search was conducted. There are so many islands in the area that the search had to be abandoned. The relatives heard of somebody who could use the pendulum to obtain information. The pendulum was just a piece of metal on a string. It was held over a map of the area and slowly moved across the map. At one spot it began to move. The relatives chartered a boat and went to that island. They found the marooned party there.

You can use a button on a string or a pendant. By holding the string with your elbow resting on a table, you can let the pendulum dangle over a map, a floor plan, a street map, or ads in a newspaper or your classified telephone directory.

When you gradually move the pendulum, be sure not to agitate it. It will agitate apparently of its own accord when it is over the answer to your question. Of course, it is not really of its own accord. It is your psychotronic detection that is being magnified. The subtle responses that you might not otherwise be aware of are given greater visibility by the lever action of the pendulum.

Practice the following Action Plan on things you already know the answer to or unimportant matters until you find you are consistently accurate. Then you know that communications have been established with the pendulum and you can use it for the "jack pot."

Action plan to obtain valuable information through the pendulum

Make a pendulum using a ring or button and a piece of string, or use a piece of jewelry on a chain such as a pendant.

Keep it on your person and near you for a few days. (This step can be shortened by holding it in your hands for a few minutes as you go to your "special room.")

Create an answer sheet with "yes" on one side, "no" on the other side and other possible answers printed clearly in between. (If the problem or information involves a map, diagram, or floor plan, use instead of answer sheet.)

Sit with your elbow on a table and the pendulum hanging quietly over the answer sheet or map.

Ask the question, directing it to the universal consciousness.

Move your arm so as not to agitate the pendulum, permitting it to hang over one part of the answer sheet or map, then another, criss-crossing, in grid fashion, until there is a sudden movement of the pendulum.

Repeat the process to be sure. When you get a consistent position or "reply" from the pendulum accept the information.

Everybody can use the pendulum accurately with practice. I have seen a young man use it to find out whom his girl friend was with that night. A salesman used it on a street map to determine the best streets to solicit that evening and his business improved. An Arizona prospector used it over his claim map and made a strike worth in the tens of thousands of dollars.

There have been many occasions when the author has used it, as over a calendar to get the right date to schedule an activity for optimum results; over an astrological chart to know a person's sign before I met him so as to have insight into how he might react to a business proposal; over a list of names of available experts to know the right one to choose.

One time I failed. I was in Tokyo on a television show with other psychics, predicting the future for the year to come. To make the show more interesting for the viewing audience, the producer said he would turn on a radio to hear the running of a steeplechase race and asked us all to pick the winner.

I did not feel comfortable about this but as it was not solving any human problems decided I would play along. I decided to use my pendulum, took it out, and held it over the list of entries and odds that was distributed to all the predictors.

As soon as I did this, all four cameras zoomed in on me. I have been on many television shows before but to have four cameras trained on my pendulum did, I confess, cause some tension. The pendulum was agitated wherever I held it. I ended up picking the wrong horse. If I could read Japanese and had just picked the favorite, I would have been better off. It won.

Once you set up communications between the pendulum and your "higher self," you are able to use any kind of psychic lever, such as the divining or dowsing rod.

The dowsing rod can be used in the field, or at home in close quarters but it is not as sensitive over small maps as the pendulum. United States troops used the dowsing rod in Vietnam to locate funneling Viet Cong. Techniques vary. To do it, just get a forked stick. Hold the forked part in each hand, the rest of the stick pointed forward. Ask your question. Move around and forward until you feel it pulling you to the object of your search.

Your hands fairly crackle with psychotronic energy. The more you realize this fact, the more energy flows. Soon it can become a bolt of energy that can knock people unconscious. The late Katherine Kuhlman developed herself as a channel for this power in the healing process, and people who came on the stage for healing collapsed into the waiting arms of attendants as this energy struck them. This same phenomenon is being repeated by other healers in the country today.

This power grows as long as it has the "agreement" of universal consciousness. The Cosmic Psychotronic Generator is then hooked up with your own mind so that whatever your desire is activated by the very force of creation itself.

Skeptics and evil-doers land in the same power-less vacuum.

Skepticism breaks the circuit in your own consciousness. Evil breaks the circuit in universal consciousness.

Believe you can. Then do *all* the good for (1) others and (2) yourself, in this order, anything you can think of.

HOW TO CREATE A BATTERY OUT OF A GLASS OF WATER WHICH THEN TAKES OVER FOR YOU

Another "lever" for hand energy is water. It is very special, as water seems to be a stage closer than solid matter to the nebulous world of ever-creating thought.

Water and electricity are both intermediate types of stages in the creative process. Magnetic and electrical phenomena are usually the easiest for beginner psychics to perform.

Albert N. was just getting interested in parapsychology and thought transference. One morning he was describing a funny cartoon to his mother. "The woman says to the psychiatrist, 'The phone is driving me crazy. It never rings'."

With that, Albert turns to the phone and says "That should do it. Ring, phone, ring." Before his mother could even begin to smile at his antics, the phone rang.

Coincidence? Fine, but listen to the conversation.

"Hello, Albert speaking."

"Albert? Oh, how did I get you? This is John. I must have dialed the wrong number."

His best friend at the university, the one most tuned in to him, had responded to Albert's mental "call."

Psychotronic energy finds paths of little resistance through water and electricity. You can use water to "command" solutions. Water is called the universal solvent. Everything dissolves in it. Problems placed in water yield solutions.

Hermes, the philosopher whose wisdom made him a god in the eyes of the Egyptians and Greeks, taught secret methods to the rulers of those countries. As the occult is de-occulted, the secrets have been uncovered and examined. They make sense in the light of modern research into psychotronics.

One of Hermes secrets was a way to get what you want using a glass of water. See what you want as you peer into the water, as if you were looking into a crystal ball into the future. Drink the water, image and all, knowing the image of your goal will enter every cell of your body and activate it toward that accomplishment.

Today we know that living cell is in touch with living cell. Activate a goal in the cells of your body and cells in human bodies everywhere hear the "call."

What kinds of problems will water help you to solve? Just about every kind. Here are just a few examples:

- Attract the right person to do some task that you want done.
- Move into a better job or position.
- Bring the right mate to your side.
- End a situation that is causing suffering and anxiety.
- Find a way to circumvent people in your way.
- Communicate with somebody even if you do not know where he is.
- Get out from under the control or demands of somebody.
- Create a flow of money to get what you need.
- Turn a weakness into strength.
- Win back a love partner you have lost.
- Bring retribution to somebody who is doing wrong.
- Get an answer to some problem that does not seem to have an answer.

To perform this Action Plan using water, you will need a glass of water, and a slice of lemon. You will perform it three times. The best time to start is before retiring at night.

Action plan to a solution activated through water

Fill a glass with water, at least half full.

Squeeze three drops of lemon into it. This acts to make the water a better conductor of energy.

Standing, hold the glass of water with the tips of your fingers of both hands, making sure the fingers are separated and not touching each other (to prevent flow of psychotronic energy from one finger into the other and insure greater flow into the water).

Turn your eyes upward to contact universal consciousness.

State your problem.

Affirm your confidence in the water as a conductor of your request for a solution.

Drink all of the water.

Repeat twice, once right after arising, and again later that day.

We have found that solutions are activated swiftly with these water techniques, usually within 72 hours.

HOW THE FINGERS CAN ACTIVATE SUPER-PSYCHOTRONIC POWER TO MAKE YOUR WISHES COME TRUE

When you keep the fingers separated, your psychotronic energy flows out through your hands to enlist outside help. When you put the tips of your fingers together, your psychotronic energy builds up your own generating system to create "inside" reinforcement.

A well-known mind course teaches a three-finger technique to trigger greater awareness. The student accepts conditioning that whenever he puts the tips of the first three fingers of either hand together, he triggers greater awareness for memory and ESP.

And it works. It works so well that it was declared illegal for a while at a Florida college where a girl student had used the three-finger technique to answer a difficult test question by reading the professor's mind. It turned out nobody else in the class got that question right because the professor had neglected to cover that ground. On questioning the young lady and discovering she had a way of reading his mind, putting the three fingers together in a test was declared prohibited.

Most teachers of this mind course explain the miraculous working of the three-finger technique as a conditioned triggering device. Pavlov's bells were a triggering device to start the flow of saliva. To bring this about all he had to do was ring the bells whenever he fed the dogs. Then the bells triggered saliva. In the three-finger technique, the student accepts the conditioning and from that time on it works.

But more is at work than conditioning. Psychotronic energy is being focused inwardly to reinforce the thought-action process.

Use the following Action Plan to increase the power in any Action Plan you use to control people, situations, circumstances, health, and luck.

Action plan to accelerate results

Perform your Action Plan.

Put your three fingers together in your "special room" or early in the Plan if no visit to the room is made.

Know that by putting your three fingers together you are activating greater energy and accelerating results of your Plan.

Accept success.

Morton D., a business consultant, was intrigued with the subject of psychotronic energy. He kept asking for more and more information about scientific research in the field.

"Why don't you stop studying it and start using it," I suggested, when I had run out of literature for him. "What do you need right now?"

"A new client," he shot back.

"Okay," I replied, "next time you have a chance to make a new client, keep these three fingers together." I held up my left hand with the tips of the thumb, forefinger, and middle finger touching.

"And . . .?"

"And, nothing. That's all there is to it."

Morton D. called me less than a week later, absolutely exultant. He had landed that new client. It was a $10,000 contract.

11

HOW YOUR EYES CAN COMMAND IRRESISTIBLE POWER TO MAKE ONE PERSON OR MANY DO YOUR BIDDING

In this chapter you learn the real power of light and how your psychotronic energy can harness this power with the help of your eyes to win admiration and support from people you don't even know. You learn how to activate a person to help you physically, intellectually, financially, or emotionally using special colors. An Action Plan enables you to trigger compliance in another person for your every wish.

When John N. Ott of the Environmental Health and Light Research Institute of Sarasota, Florida, first became interested in the effects of light on health, he discovered the cells of grass behaved differently under different color lights. When his search took him further up the evolutionary ladder to animal cells, he again found that changing the color of light used in his microphotography could cause radical changes within the cells. He could increase their metabolic activity. He could even kill them.

This led quickly to the inescapable conclusion that there was some mysterious link between light and the mental state, as well as physical health of human beings.

The mystery is less a mystery today than it was more than a decade ago when Ott was making his discovery. It is largely agreed today that light entering through the eyes causes nerve impulses that go to the lower brain and to the pituitary gland. This gland triggers the release of certain hormones. These hormones could well be the mysterious link between light and mental and physical health. In fact, there is expanded study going on today in what is recognized as the retinal-hypothalamic endocrine *system.*

In this chapter we will discuss how this eye-mind-body relationship is now being used to control conditions not only within ourselves but within other people, even though they are a distance away.

EYE CONTACT AND THE CONTROL YOU CAN EXERT WITH IT

A mother is angry at her child. She points her finger at him. Her eyes are open in a staring way. "Put that ash tray back where you got it." she orders. The child looks into her wide open eyes–and then obeys.

People have been controlling other people with eye contact for ages, without knowing what they were doing. Parent-child, boss-worker, man-woman.

Magicians in the Hermes tradition of yesteryear used a magnetic eye bath to improve the power of their eyes to control situations. They boiled a basin of water and then stared into it, imagining the face of the person they wished to control and sending the orders they wished obeyed. The following day they would bathe their eyes in this water by dipping their face into the basin, then opening their eyes while under the water and rolling them in all directions, repeating seven times. This eyebath was said to enhance eye control and improve clairvoyance.

Modern knowledge of the effects of relaxation make this an even more powerful tool than the magnetized water.

Nora G. had started a book with a colleague at the school where they taught. In the middle of the project, he accepted a job with another school thousands of miles away. For years, Nora corresponded with this man trying to encourage him to continue with the manuscript, but he claimed he was too busy.

Since his cooperation was essential to the project, Nora was stymied. This had been her big chance for educational recognition. Then she learned about the powers of the mind at the relaxed level. She used psychotronics to try to influence her friend to resume the book-writing project. She relaxed, she saw him responding positively. Within two weeks she received a letter from his saying how anxious he now was to resume the project and how successful he knew it would be.

Nora's success was due to the following Action Plan:

Action plan to make a person do your bidding

Go to your "special room."

Relax deeply.

See the person you wish to influence about ten feet away.

Make the image larger until you are able to see his or her eyes clearly.

Look into the person's eyes, opening up the aperture of your eyes as you do.

Explain what you want done and why—making logical, reasonable points.

End your session.

Repeat several times a day.

THE PROS AND CONS OF MAKING OTHER PEOPLE DO YOUR BIDDING

There have always been two classes of people: those who give orders and those who carry them out.

Man has perfected his organizing ability from simple family organization to tribe to country—and from tradesman-apprentice to huge corporations and complicated conglomerates.

There are many books written on managing people, getting them to do what you as their supervisor want them to do. All of these books are based on psychological precepts. None that I know of are based on psychotronic precepts.

Yet, leaders have been using these psychotronic precepts, albeit unwittingly. Bring these precepts out in the open, give them a methodology, use them under conscious control, and you have a powerful force to control people.

The power of this force makes it dangerous. Just the way guns, bombs, and now atomic weaponry put dangerous power into the hands of men and governments, so psychotronics places dangerous power into the hands of those individuals reading this book or other books that will be published on this subject as science advances. You have a great responsibility to use the power wisely.

When a foreman instructs a welder to halt work on one ship part and to begin to work on another, he is doing what he believes is right to maintain the flow of production in accordance with priorities. The welder may not see any sense in leaving a job unfinished, yet he accedes to the instructions of his superior.

The process we call life does not provide us with clear cut priorities. It is not possible to measure our desires against some logical standards to check out their priority. So we do whatever we think we should do. We follow our will.

We also enjoin another to follow our will. There's the rub. He has a will, too. Unlike the welder he has no fear of being fired by you. You are not his boss. In the process we call life, there are no bosses. Each person follows his own leanings, his own best judgment, his own will. So there are conflicts.

Life is one conflict of wills after another. No author can expect to write a successful piece of fiction without conflict in it. Life without conflict just does not hold interest for a reader. It falls flat. It is unreal. The resolution of billions of wills may be what life is all about.

Dictators try to resolve wills by dominance. "My will, not yours." Occasionally there are benevolent dictators whose will seems to express understanding, compassion, and the need for others to move freely within the confines of the ruler's dictates. Then, occasionally there is a Hitler.

Examine benevolence and you see a quality of love and attunement. It is as if the benevolent dictator's will is in tune with a larger universal will.

You have two paths. You can choose to be a Hitler. All the way to the end. Or you can choose to dictate to others in a way that is in tune with the benevolent universe. The Action Plans in this chapter will work in both cases. But the end will be different.

HOW TO ATTUNE YOUR WILL SO THAT WHAT YOU WANT IS WHAT THE UNIVERSE SUPPORTS

In an earlier chapter, we aligned our psychotronic generator with the Cosmic Psychotronic Generator. This gave us more power. However, whenever a generating plant adds power to the line it must go through a phasing operation. The power introduced into the line must be in phase with the power already there.

The Action Plan that follows has the same purpose. It places your psychotronic power in phase with the power of universal consciousness.

Some may recognize it as a type of meditation. I meditate every morning for a few minutes, in my own way. Hopefully, by meditating I attune my consciousness to the universal consciousness, or God.

If I am totally out of tune, my will could conceivably be diametrically opposed to His will. However, if I am totally in tune, my will could very well be identical with His will. So when I go to my alpha level and work on a woman in New York who is faced with a hip operation for her arthritis, and the pain leaves her, I am hopefully not interfering. And if somebody asks me to forsee the optimum use for a piece of land and I decline, I am hopefully not rude.

When I go to my "special room" to influence a person to do my will, I know that there is a better chance that, because of my morning meditation, I am using my psychotronic power in phase with the universal psychotronic power. And just in case I have gone out of phase, I add this proviso to my "instructions" to the person I am controlling: "Do it if it is the universal will."

When you meditate, all you are really doing is "nothing." It takes a certain know-how to do nothing. However, you now have this know-how. Meditation takes know-how in relaxing body and mind. You know how. Meditation takes know-how in being aware of universal consciousness. You know how.

Meditation takes know-how in becoming a loving part of universal consciousness. Read this Action Plan and you will know how to do this, too. Then do it.

Action plan to place your psychotronic power in phase with that of the universe

Go to your "special room" and relax deeply.

Visualize a light descending from the skylight and enveloping you.

Create a rheostat in your imagination that permits you to brighten the light by merely turning an imagined dial.

Brighten the light by slowly turning the imaginary dial.

Feel yourself bathed in this bright light, understanding it to be cosmic light that heightens your awareness and intelligence.

Become aware only of the *here* and *now.*

Be.

End your session feeling love and oneness with universal consciousness.

This Action Plan has two effects. It attunes your will to the universal will and purpose. This means that when you seek to have others do your will, you are more likely to be right in your intent. Secondly, it increases your chances of having arrived at an intelligent decision.

HOW TO UP YOUR IQ AND WIN ADMIRATION AND SUPPORT FROM OTHERS

Psychologists for generations have been claiming that intelligence is a factor of heredity not environment. Recently, many psychologists have decided to take another look at this.

They find that self-concept affects intelligence. Students in socio-economically deprived areas, whose teachers expect poor scholastic performance, tend to live up to their teachers dismal hopes for them. When something is done to change this, like the experiment that moved children from a Boston elementary school to a Harvard University classroom, the students live up to the new expectations. Slow learners and under achievers become even better than average.

In October 1976 findings by researchers at Hull University in

England and Princeton University in New Jersey revealed that one of the most respected British educational psychologists of his time—the late Sir Cyril Burt—had apparently rigged his statistics to support his belief that intelligence is hereditary. This belief became accepted largely due to his research. Now this theory is being seriously re-examined in the light of new evidence to the contrary.

The author experienced a rise in his own Intelligence Quotient as he engaged in consciousness expanding procedures, now known as Psychotronics. In 1943 he received 144 on a standard intelligence test. Around 1965, attempting to enter the Mensa Society he scored 148, not enough to make membership restricted to the top two percent of the population so measured. Then in 1973 he took a concentrated 40-hour training in subjective use of the mind, again took the standard intelligence test required for Mensa membership, and this time made it with room to spare.

The more you meditate as in the above Action Plan, the more you open your mind to more intelligent functioning.

It is the person with superior intelligence that people look to for guidance. No test is necessary. The consciousness that is enlightened is instinctively listened to, respected, obeyed. You become in control of others even in spite of yourself. Do you realize what this new understanding about human intelligence means to you?

You are not a stupid person no matter how many times arrogant people have "put you down." And that includes your parents and teachers. You are even more intelligent than the average person. Just how intelligent are you?

You are as intelligent as you agree to be. You can agree to be a stupid person. Some of you maybe have done so years ago. You can change that agreement with yourself and make a new agreement. Do you agree to be a person of superior intelligence? Can you see yourself smart, wise, and witty? "Agreement" means acceptance of such a picture.

Do this Action Plan to trigger your own acceptance of a better self-image and to permit a new agreement with yourself for superior intelligence.

Action plan to trigger a higher IQ

Go to your "special room" and relax.

See yourself admired by others.

Perform the previous Action Plan using the rheostat to turn up the light.

Again see yourself admired by others.

Repeat the rheostat Action Plan.

Now see yourself proclaimed a leader by others. Use appropriate pictures that fit your life style. These could be:

- You are a hero carried on the shoulders of your colleagues.
- You occupy a huge office.
- You are being given a testimonial dinner; you hear the speeches honoring you.
- You have a dressing room with a star on the door.

End your Action by affirming: "There is no limit to the intelligence I have access to. I am becoming more and more of a genius with every mental step I take."

HOW TO GIVE MENTAL COMMANDS IN FORCEFUL "TECHNICOLOR"

In Chapter 5 we discussed color and its effects. We are now ready to review this in the light of our progress and to begin to use color in Action Plans to enhance the action and expedite the Plan.

You are able to invite a person (in your imagination) to enter your special Action Plan room and then to have a talk that will change the intentions of that person to conform with your own intentions.

As psychotronic engineers get into the study of Kirlian photography, they are finding a significance to color in the human aura, or psychotronic radiation. With this knowledge, you are able to color your mental images "successful."

Let's reexamine just what colors are useful to add power to your mental commands. We will go from the red side of the spectrum to the deep purples.

Red is the energy color. It spurs to action. If a person is depressed, apathetic, disinterested, lazy, you can spur him to action in your behalf with the use of red.

Orange is a social color. It encourages mixing, joining and it enhances salesmanship. If you wish to spur a loner to become a more effective member of a group, orange is the color.

Yellow acts upon the brain and nervous system. If a person is nervous about working with you or is intellectually unsure, use yellow.

Green is a peaceful, healing color. If a person is pained by aspects of your work, you can project peace and growth by using green.

Blue is a loving color. If a person feels hostility to you, plan a proposal, send blue.

Violet and purple are uplifting colors from a spiritual point of view. If a person has reservations about the ethics or morals of your good intentions, send violet.

Color all commands—true. Be honest and sincere in your strivings for the common good and you are bound to move whomever you wish to do your bidding.

Here is the Action Plan that uses these colors to add force to your mental control over others.

Action plan to add force to your command through color

Go to your special place and relax.

Invite the person you wish to activate.

Surround that person with the appropriate light, as you present your reasons and your wishes.

Complete Action Plan as before.

You have every right to attempt to convince others to do your bidding, if you feel that it is for the common good. Your gut feeling that this is so is especially dependable if you use the white light on yourself frequently.

White is the total spectrum of light—all colors. It is universal light in balance. It can maintain you in balance with universal goals of problem-solving and growth. It helps your psychotronic power to be "in phase" with universal psychotronic power. So it is advisable to perform the Action Plan for phasing before you decide to force your commands through color.

THE LAW OF KARMA, UNDERLINED IN PSYCHOTRONICS

St. Paul said, "Be not deceived, God is not mocked. For whatsoever a man soweth, that shall he also reap." In the Hindu world this is called the law of Karma. The law states that doing good begets a good reward, doing wrong begets its own reward, otherwise known as punishment.

When you look at the law of Karma, or at St. Paul's sow-reap analogy, in the light of psychotronics, the operation of this good-begets-good principle is better understood.

One does need to accept a concept of a human-like god weighing every deed on the scale of good and evil and then meting out its reward or punishment. Instead, one sees that the individual's energy of consciousness triggers a response in the universal energy of consciousness of which the individual is part. So the individual, being part, is involved in the reward or in the punishment that he himself has triggered.

Cleve Backster hooked a plant up to a polygraph (lie detector) and got a reaction every time he thought of injuring the plant. The plant picked up his thought and showed a reaction on the meter even before he picked up the matches to burn the leaf or the scissors to cut it. However, if he did not really mean to injure the plant and just thought it to get a read-out on the meter, there was no reaction. The plant seemed to know when he meant it, and when not. Motive is the key.

There is no fooling universal consciousness with synthetic thought or feelings. The true underlying motive is what registers and what determines the reward or punishment. This has been long understood by preachers and moralizers. Now it is a scientific fact.

For our own good, we need to control other people with psychotronic power, not as a master does his slaves, but as a statesman among men.

WHAT ACTUALLY HAPPENS WITHIN THE PERSON YOU CONTROL

A man sees a vineyard. The arbor is laden with grapes. They are tempting. He imagines what they taste like. He senses their succulence. He walks over, picks some and pops the first one into his mouth, followed by others.

A child touches a pot on the kitchen range. He immediately pulls his hand away. It was scorching hot.

In the case of the grapes, the voluntary act was preceded by thought. In the case of the hot stove, there was an involuntary act that required no thought.

The hypnotist can create a desired behavior in a subject. This kind of control becomes automatic. The person so controlled, even though no longer in a hypnotic state, will carry out the instructions in an involuntary manner that requires no thought. He behaves as an automaton.

The psychotronic engineer–which you now are–can create a desired behavior in a subject but it is not automatic. The subject does so voluntarily after appropriate thought.

Both the hypnotist and the psychotronic engineer have a responsibility to use their power for good. But the psychotronic engineer might be in a better ethical position. He is getting the consent of his subject at a superconscious level, using reason. True, he is bypassing normal conditioned responses and communicating in a subjective realm, but it is still valid communication. It is where most of man's communications used to be before language was invented, and where communication in most of nature still takes place.

Eye contact needs to be on a face to face basis in hypnotism. You will see the hypnotist increase the aperture of his own eyes slightly as he holds the gaze of his subject. Eye contact in psychotronics is held at a subjective, or imaginary level. The hypnotist is using his eyes to induce submission. The psychotronic engineer is using his eyes to induce agreement in what you might describe as a telepathic way. If you were controlled by a hypnotists's power, you would not know why you took off your shoes at high noon. If you were controlled by psychotronic power, you would stop to think at high noon about taking off your shoes. If there was a valid reason–and there could be one supplied in this case–you would then take them off, knowing exactly why you were doing so, but possibly not knowing just exactly how you received the information.

In each case the subject can resist. In the case of the hypnotized subject, taking off the shoes in public may be a terrifying thing to do. So the subject fumbles with the shoes not knowing why and resists taking them off. In the case of the subject being motivated through your psychotronic power, there might be also a Victorian-like conditioning against taking off the shoes in front of other people. The subject then would seek some other way to accommodate the purpose you wanted to achieve. In each case, resisting would cause a discomfort.

Sydney L. was a junior in a private high school where the author gave a condensed course in hypnotism. He was a good subject and cooperated quite well in various demonstrations. However, in one session, to give the class a feeling of a conditioned response, I put them all into a light trance-like state (alpha) and then gave each a command to perform when I said the word "Philadelphia."

I ended the session and began to talk about the trip I would soon take. "I'll be visiting Philadelphia." At the sound of that word, shoes came off, books dropped, students jumped up and the commands I previously gave were carried out—except for Sidney L. I had commanded him to turn off the classroom lights. His resistance was welcomed, because I wanted a student or two to describe their feelings while "resisting."

"Do you feel uncomfortable?" I asked Sidney. "Not at all," he replied.

"Would it make you feel any better if you turned the lights off now?"

"Of course not."

I dropped the matter. In a few minutes the bell rang, the class was over and the students filed out. One student turned off the lights. Guess who?

Compare this to the case of Helen P. She had learned to use her psychotronic power. She wanted to put up a fence between her property and that of her neighbor, Ralph S., as people were using the two properties as a shortcut. She felt Ralph should share the cost. She did an Action Plan and later approached him about sharing the cost of the project. He refused outright. He said he did not want to spend the money.

Helen repeated the Action Plan several times over the next week. One Sunday she was watering the lawn and Ralph walked over to her.

"I think you are right about the fence," he said. "Suppose you buy the materials and I do the installation."

Of course, she agreed. Labor was the larger part of the cost. Her Action Plan was creating a problem for Ralph. He reversed the outcome to solve that problem.

Resistance in psychotronic work is usually due to the fact that problems are being created. Commands should be given in such a way that the solutions they provide are free of secondary problems.

THE USE OF TRIGGERING DEVICES TO GET YOUR WAY

"Mr. Stone, can you help me?"

Shirley W. was a student in my university ESP class which she was limping out of.

"I seem to have sprained my ankle playing tennis this morning. It is very painful."

"What kind of beverage do you enjoy?"

She seemed surprised. "Well . . . ice tea, I guess."

"Every time you sip ice tea slowly, it will hasten healing."

It was two days before I saw Shirley.

"Thanks," she said. "I made ice tea when I got home. It took three hours instead of the three days I expected."

"Don't thank me," I replied. "I didn't do it; you did."

Notice I did not tell Shirley what beverage to drink. That would be prescribing. Actually it did not matter what beverage was involved. So I let her "prescribe." Then after she left I went to my "special room," sprayed on an imaginary pain killer, applied a ligament and small bone corrector" and "saw" the ankle improving with each sip of ice tea.

The ice tea acted as a triggering device for the healing. Understanding this will help you to accept the amazing results that triggering devices can produce when you use your eyes to "see" them at work in other ways.

Mark J. and Dan L. shared an apartment. They had different jobs and different hours so they did not see too much of each other, but whenever they did Mark had plenty to say to Dan about the way he left his belongings scattered about and never did his share of housekeeping. Dan was unmoved by the encounters and Mark began to look for another place to live.

One of Mark's co-workers told him about a mind controlling course. He took it. He then began to use what he learned to solve the problem he had with lazy Dan. He did this by going to his "special place," imagining Dan and seeing Dan getting more and more appreciative of the apartment's cleanliness and neatness with every step he took inside. He used Dan's step as a triggering device. He also surrounded Dan in a red light of energy.

Within a few days, scattered shirts and newspapers began to disappear. Dishes were no longer left in the sink. A week later Dan actually got out the vacuum cleaner for the first time. And Mark stopped looking for another apartment.

Your Action Plan is similar:

Action plan to trigger compliance

Go to your "special room."

Visualize the person as if actually there.

Eye the person and give the logical, reasonable argument for complying with your wishes.

See this compliance beginning when a triggering device is activated (see below). See more and more compliance taking place with each repeated activation of the triggering device.

End your session with a statement that you wish this compliance only if it furthers the universal purpose, solving problems without creating new ones.

You can use as your triggering device any simple motion, sound, sight, taste, or other sensory input. Some additional triggering devices might be:

- Noticing a member of the opposite sex
- Using an eating utensil
- Climbing stairs
- Stepping on the car accelerator
- Talking
- Breathing
- Hearing the clock strike

Coaches can trigger better and better performance by team members. Lovers can trigger better and better fulfillment in the love act by their partner. Employers can trigger more and more efficient work by their personnel. Teachers can trigger better and better learning by their students.

You can use this triggering device on yourself, too. See yourself in your "special room" as if in a mirror. Hold eye contact with yourself. Convince yourself of the reasonableness of the improvement you wish to take place or the activity you wish yourself to perform. See yourself moving in this direction every time you drink a glass of water or do some other common activity which then becomes a triggering device.

Artists can trigger greater ability. Writers can trigger more creativity. Salesmen can trigger more confidence and enthusiasm.

Before you begin the next chapter, decide how you would like to improve your work, profession, or social life. Do an Action Plan in which you present the reasons, and then see yourself triggering improvement many times a day.

Accept my congratulations in advance.

12

HOW TO USE PSYCHOTRONIC POWER TO PREDICT THE FUTURE–YOURS OR ANYONE'S

In this chapter you learn how to use the dream faculty to get answers about the future, and how to get mental pictures you can trust that foretell the future as if you had a built-in crystal ball. And in this chapter is revealed the ultimate secret–how to use psychotronic power to change unwanted events you see in the future.

If our consciousness is part of a larger consciousness which we call the universal consciousness, why can't we pick up intelligence anywhere, past, present or future?

The answer is we can. Let's talk about the future. Will there be an earthquake? Will the stock market go up? Will I meet the great love of my life? You can answer these questions, using your psychotronic energy.

Take the first question–about a possible earthquake. Animals know the answer. A zoo in California near the San Andreas Fault is making a study of how their animals' behavior changes days before a quake. Animals have psychotronic energy. They are relaxed and at their subjective or alpha level of mind more than we are. An "uneasiness" is received by them without their being conscious of what is happening.

You are able to go animals one better. You are able to receive earthquake information at will, anytime you want it, and to perceive it at a greater distance into the future. In this chapter we will go into the way this is easily done.

How about the second question: will the stock market go up?

The author was asked to speak at a Rotary luncheon recently. It was early in January and they wanted me to make predictions on the economy, especially the stock market. I know absolutely nothing about the stock market but it was easy for me to "see" that it was going to go up rather sharply that very month, that it would suffer three setbacks during the year and I mentioned the months in which these would occur.

"Will it go above the Dow Jones 1,000 level?" asked a Rotarian.

"No" I replied, "It will reach that mark a few times but not go above it."

These predictions were 100 percent accurate. The first few times this had happened I was quite surprised. I felt I was guessing. Yet how could guesses be that accurate? In this chapter we will provide the method to "guess" accurately.

And what about the third question–the great love? Yes, in this chapter we will go into how to determine just when this event will happen in your life.

You can accurately predict all matters that affect your survival or the survival of other people. Survival depends on natural phenomena, on money, and on love.

THE SECRET BEHIND ACCURATE PREDICTING

When you live in Hawaii as I do, where nearly half of the population is of Japanese ancestry, you naturally develop an interest to see Japan. As this desire was growing in me, I began to visualize it happening. Soon I received an invitation from a Japanese magazine to make predictions about Japan's financial and political affairs. I did so using the techniques in this chapter. These were published and turned out to be 85% correct.

This only whetted my appetite to visit Tokyo, so I began to use my psychotronic power. My hands pointed to Japanese restaurants, my eyes probed Japanese visitors. I visualized myself in Tokyo.

In just a few weeks I received an invitation to visit Tokyo and make predictions for 1976. My expenses were fully paid by a television station. They tested me on the two hour program with a variety of predictions. For instance, they brought a young man onto the stage.

"What is his future?" they asked me through an interpreter. I hooked up with the Cosmic Psychotronic Generator and instantly got the information that he was to start a new venture, that it would take him off that island, that it would be successful, but that it would not be permanent.

While the interpreter was relating what I had said, the man's face broke out in smiles. He was a Japanese movie star about to leave the island to make a big, new film. All I was telling him that he did not already know was that his new film would be a success. I later found out that it was one of his best.

Our detection of information "psychically"–that is, by means other than our five senses–is going on all the time. But we edit it. We discard this thought or that thought, because we did not deduce it from some input of our eyes, ears, nose, taste, or touch. Since it is not acquired in this manner, we conclude it is a guess. Information obtained psychically is therefore quickly identified as guesswork and discarded.

Those of us who train our psychic functioning so that it comes under control are struck with the same doubts and suspicions when psychic information is received. "I'm afriad to say it–I'm just guessing." This is the normal feeling for psychic accuracy.

Really, the only thing that changes when you begin to function as a psychic is that you are detecting information that you want when you want it, without the use of the five senses.

The information you receive psychically "feels" the same as any other information you receive. No bells ring. No siren sounds. No voices whisper in your ear. "This is God returning your call. Now, about that question you asked." It just does not happen that way.

Get ready to accept your guesses. Prepare yourself to become a more frequent guesser. Then expect a miracle: a parade of accurate guesses. This is the secret behind accurate predicting—*trust your guesses.*

If your attitude is one of doubt and suspicion, you will come up with information that is doubtful and suspicious. If your attitude is one of confidence, you will come up with information that you can be confident in.

George A. had taken a commercial course leading to the development of ESP. He had done so with reservations that he could ever become psychic. When he proved to be fairly accurate at the conclusion of the course he "wrote it off" as lucky guesswork. But he still had hopes. So, he enrolled in the graduate course—an advanced workshop for graduates of the course he took.

The instructor was in his closing remarks at the conclusion of this workship when George raised his hand. "I can't do it," he said to the instructor. "I just can't do it."

Perhaps somewhat miffed by the injection of this negativity at that point in the workshop, the instructor commanded, "Stand up, George!" George stood up, wondering what was about to happen.

"I have a card in my pocket. On it are the ailments of Mary Smith, age 32, of Fifth Avenue, New York. I am going to walk toward you, before I reach you, I want you to tell me the nature of those ailments."

As George sputtered his protest, the instructor began to walk down the aisle toward him.

"Cancer of the chest; left arm amputated," blurted out George.

The instructor took the card out of his pocket and showed it to George. George's eyes opened wide. He was absolutely correct.

The instructor had not given George time to inject doubt and to therefore come up with doubtful results. He had to trust whatever came to him. When you have a consciousness of trust, you resonate with trustworthy information.

PRECOGNITIVE DREAMS AND HOW TO CONTROL THEM

The great psychic Edgar Cayce did all of his detection of information at a distance and forward and backward in time by going into a light sleep. He talked in this sleep, had no recollection of what he said, and so had a secretary take down the information.

Cayce believed that the spirit of man, including his mental ability, is a part of the "whole great spirit." So all answers can come through him, through his mental functioning.

Dreams have long been recognized as a source of prophecy. Ancient oracles did much of their divination through dreams. A language of dreams is different than the language of the dreamer. It is usually in symbols and pictures that require interpretation. The first dream "dictionary" was written about the year 150 A.D. by Artemidorus, a Greek psychic. It was four large volumes. Dream books are more compact today but dreams are no less baffling.

If we could remember and understand every dream we have, we would recognize in each dream some valuable information about our survival. Dreams hold a mirror up to us and say, "This is what your attitude is," or "This is what you are doing." The message is that we had better change, or else. Even knowing this message, changing is not that easy. We tend to brush warnings aside even from our doctor.

One woman interpreted a dream to mean that if she continued being promiscuous, she would contract a veneral disease. She ignored the advice and the dream came true. A man interpreted his dream to mean that if he was not more pleasant to his fellow employees, he would lose his job. He wasn't, and he did.

Those who value advice, take it. If you are interested in the advice your dreams have for you, especially regarding your future, here is how to control the dreaming function in a practical way.

THE PROPHETIC DREAM–HOW TO HAVE, REMEMBER, AND UNDERSTAND IT

You can order a dream.

You can order it more easily than filling out a mail order form. Psychologists and psychiatrists have largely ignored this even though a few of their number have reported professionally on the positive results. Commercial courses have taken up the procedure and formalized it as part of their mental control programs.

The key to ordering a dream and then having it is *necessity*. If the dream you want is to help you know the cause of a health problem in yourself or somebody else, such a dream is assured. If the dream is to help you improve a financial condition, you will have such a dream. If the dream will answer a love question, it is on its way.

If the dream concerns what will happen in the future, your motive must be more than curiosity. Your motive must involve health, money, love or other factors essential to your survival. Curiosity might even interfere with your survival. Remember how it killed the cat? Desiring a dream about the future so that it can help solve some problem, assures such a dream.

Here is the Action Plan to have it:

Action plan to have a problem-solving dream about the future

Retire in the usual way.

Before falling asleep, when you feel relaxed and drowsy . . .

Tell your mind–as if it had a personality of its own–that you want to have a dream to solve a specific problem.

Identify the problem, stating it in words.

Add that you want to not only have such a dream but that you want to remember it and understand it.

Go to sleep.

You may wake up some time during the night after a dream. Sleep with pen and paper near by so you can write it down. Dreams have a way of slipping away with time. Capture it on paper. The more you write down, the more you will remember, and the more valuable the information. Or, you may wake up in the morning with such a dream. Again, write it down even though you think it is so vivid you will never forget it.

Arthur R. had a gallbladder attack. The pain was so excruciating he had to go to the hospital where x-rays confirmed the stones. He decided to postpone the immediate operation recommended by his physician.

Soon after his release from the hospital he had another attack. This time x-rays could not pick up any more stones. Still his physician recommended that the gall bladder be removed, but because he felt there was a chance that the last of the stones had been passed, Arthur once again refused.

After returning home from the hospital, he could still feel slight pains that seemed to indicate all was not normal. Would he have another attack? He decided to ask for a dream that would fortell what he might expect.

He did the Action Plan above and woke up the next morning with a vivid dream that he was sitting beside his apartment house swimming pool on a sunny day, but could not swim because the pool was being cleaned. The manager had a long broom and was sweeping the sludge from the bottom of the pool toward the outlet pipe.

What this said to Arthur was that in the months ahead he would not have any attack such as he had twice before but that he would have discomfort as, not stones, but sand or sludge was cleaned from the gall bladder and passed through the small ducts. This proved to be exactly so.

Using this Action Plan on the edge of sleep is the best timing. However, some of us are not fully relaxed if there is a purpose such as this on our mind. So the edge of sleep never comes. For others, the edge of sleep comes so fast and so precipitously that we are over the edge and morning comes with the Action Plan missed.

A procedure to follow in this case would be to retire, then as soon as you are in bed, take yourself through the imaging procedure of going to your "special room," relaxing and then performing the rest of the Action Plan.

HOW TO SEE THE FUTURE PLAYED BEFORE YOU ON A STAGE IN FULL VIEW

You have a "special place" that is far more special than you imagine. Even though you may have already used it to control people, to cause wealth to flow to you, to bring luck and a better life, you still have only a bare inkling of its real potential.

There is nothing that can be kept from you in the past, present, or future, near or far. In a few pages I will tell you how to use this special place to see future events as if they were being played on a stage in front of you.

But before I do I need your wholehearted attention. The procedure is done with psychotronic energy. By now you know that it is energy that can be used for good or bad.

Let's look in on a voodoo-type practitioner, perhaps in Haiti. He has taken some loam and wax, mixed it with water, and kneaded the pulp into the shape of a doll. While it is still soft, he injects fluid from top to bottom. He may include a drop or two of his own blood or sperm. He seals the aperture, rubs the doll with both hands and blows on it as if imbuing it with the breath of life. He now mumbles over and over again the name of the person the doll represents.

He is now ready to do his dirty work. Whatever he does to the doll—like stick a pin through it—he is projecting to his victim. But . . .

Suppose he hesitates and has second thoughts about it. Either he thinks maybe he should not do it because it would not serve the cause of justice. Or he thinks maybe he cannot do it, because his power is gone, or he never had it, or whatever. What then? Will it work? I'd bet against it.

Or take the white magician. He is sitting in a unity prayer group seeing a person with a critical illness healthy, seeing that person perfect. Time and time again it has worked. The person recovers from his critical illness. This time the white magician makes a negative remark to the group like, "The poor guy is too far gone." Another healing? I'd bet against it.

Psychotronics does its white magic or black magic successfully only when there is little time for doubt. So I remind you that for good or bad, the factor of doubt acts on psychotronic energy as an electrical resistance acts on electrical energy.

Since physical laws do not explain how our mind can transcend space or time, doubt has a way of being especially annoying in these applications.

Take space. While I was learning to project my intelligence across space, I asked a colleague to test me with a person he knew a distance away who had some ailment. This was stacking the deck in a way because detecting health information, it being so close to the prime necessity—survival, is the easiest information to get, through walls, or across vast distances. My colleague gave me the name of a person about five thousand miles away.

"The right ear," I said suddenly.

"What about it?"

"Crazy," I exclaimed, "It's three times bigger than the left ear." Then after a pause, "I think it's just being big to get my attention. I'm going to check it out."

I projected my awareness inside the ear and the ear drum had a big perforation in it. I sewed it up. When I ended my psychotronic session, my colleague confirmed that hearing in the right ear of this person was the major problem. We both smiled.

One of the cases I gave another colleague was the late Dr. Paul Bragg, the famous physical hygienist and former associate of Bernarr MacFadden. I used initials just in case the student recognized the name. Bragg, then 92, had recently fallen and was recovering from a broken bone in his foot which he was treating by natural means. This particular colleague was a reluctant seer. He had his doubts. But he played along.

"He's got a big crop of graying hair. And I see him in a rain forest." That was Bragg all right. Natural living, close to nature.

"What else?" I asked encouragingly.

"He looks good for his age. I don't see any outside problems. I am going to go inside him now."

A smile came over his face.

"What do you see?" I asked curiously.

"His stomach is green."

I swallowed my guffaw, turning it into a cough. "Fine, keep going."

He did not spot the little bone in his foot but I was convinced this man picked up on Paul Bragg's looks, environment, and penchant for salads and all green, alive foods. He was psychic, but the ingredient of doubt prevented total psychic functioning.

Doubt has a way of dogging your steps. Some two years later when I had seen forward and backward in time accurately scores of times and had seen through walls, across continents and into bodies accurately again and again, I was attending a psychotronic workshop and we were asked to pair off and work a case or two. Being tested again by a colleague triggered my doubts once again.

I turned to the colleague sitting next to me, a young man from the Mid-west, and asked, "Will *you* go first?" I did not give him an alternative.

"Why don't you?"

He gave *me* no alternative. I was frightened. I was just as frightened then as when I did this the first time years ago. I had done this scores of times since then, but they were not tests. This was a test. What if one of my peers witnessed me—a much publicized and heralded psychic—fail!

He gave me the initials, address, sex and age of a 12-year old boy back in his home town.

"He's blond. Quite short."

"Yes," replied my partner in a noncommital tone.

"One of those," I said to myself. "He's going to play it straight and not give me any encouragement. Or else, I've already blown it."

"In fact," I continued, "he's too small and too light in weight. He's undernourished. It's not because he's not given enough to eat.

It's something else. Let me check him out. I need to check his blood. I think that's where the problem is."

I took his silence as condescendance and proceeded. A few moments later, he asked, "What are you doing now?"

"Sure, it's his blood. It's so full of garbage that it can't properly feed his body with nutrients from food. I'm now filtering his blood and screening out all those damn impurities. What a mess!" I continued my subjective blood washing. "OK I'm going to end my session."

"Don't you want to check out the rest of his body?"

"No. He's all fixed up." I ended my session, afraid to hear whether I was right or wrong.

My friend was smiling. "You're great," he said. "Small for age, blond, undernourished. And from time to time we have to put him on a kidney machine to clean his blood. He has a kidney problem."

I was right. But I was not right enough. The whole process of being tested was so painful that I cut short the examination and wound up treating the symptom rather than the cause. If I had not let my doubts hurry me I would have spotted the malfunctioning kidneys.

I have no Action Plan to offer you that dissolves doubt. It is the prime enemy. Success is its antidote. Practice leads to its eventual conquest.

A scientific study of psychotronics enhances expectation and belief at the expense of doubt. If you can comprehend scientific journals and papers, they are excellent reading fare to build up confidence and stifle doubt. It is not the purpose of this book to supply this scientific information but rather how people in all walks of life and all stages of educational background can utilize psychotronic energy for solid benefits.

Let me just say this. Desiring to function in a psychic way causes the mind to operate from brain centers that are not ordinarily used in intellectual matters. Here the brain functions at predominantly ten cycles per second. Our mind seems then to become "resonant" to the information desired, not at the standard physical sensory level of sight and sound, but in some other way. Yet this other way often appears as sight and sound. Accuracy here is on the same level as accuracy at the physical level, especially with practice.

We know through experience that valuable information, especially information related to survival, is strongly impressed on matter.

This impression of survival information is also quite strongly impressed on cell life, most strongly on brain cells. Maybe we "read" matter. Maybe we "read" other people's brain cells, or other types of cells.

The more we practice this ten cycle or alpha brain functioning the better we are able to project our consciousness subjectively, instead of through the physical senses, and to perceive survival information needed. We become in effect, psychic investigators.

Now, that's as far as I care to go in trying to explain what happens. Are you ready to make it happen? Then let's put doubt aside—and expect a psychotronic miracle.

Action plan to see the future

Go to your "special place" and be expectant.

Relax deeply in any way that is satisfying to you.

Create an imaginary screen about 25 degrees above the horizontal.

Ask the question you wish to be revealed regarding the future.

Repeat mentally that the answer is vital to you to help solve a human problem.

Wait expectantly watching the screen.

Create a perpetual calendar in your imagination, located next to your screen.

Move the calendar forward in time as you continue to watch the screen expectantly.

Cease moving the calendar the moment you begin to see activity on your screen.

Observe the activity, noting the vital information you need regarding yourself or others.

The eye is basically a receiver, converter and transmitter of energy. Light energy is received, converted into optic nerve energy, and transmitted for interpretation by the brain.

When you turn your eyes upward and visualize, the process of receiving, converting, and transmitting is carried on at a nonphysical level. You might say that it is the spirit that senses. The nonphysical component of you receives, converts, and transmits at a level where time and distance does not limit.

In psychotronics, you are not asked to turn your eyes upward and look at things in another dimension. Hardly anybody would know where they were or what they were doing. This could be like finding their way in a way-less place. Instead, you are asked to look *desirously* and expectantly using an Action Plan. This desire tunes you to the information wherever it is. This expectancy draws it to you.

HOW TO CHANGE WHAT YOU SEE IN THE FUTURE

If what you see in the future is not what you feel is good, there is a chance that you can change it before it happens. It can involve you, or other people, or both.

Sometimes the cause and effect relationship has been "set" beyond anyone's power to change. For instance, the sinking of the Titanic through collision with an iceberg early in this century was forseen psychically by a number of people. Some persons dreamed it. Artists drew it. Novelists wrote stories about it. But nobody could prevent the tragedy.

We have not progressed far enough in this field of psychotronics to know when conditions are "set" beyond change or not. In the next chapter we will discuss some devices that are now being used in psychotronic research which might extend our "sensing" to be able to make such a determination. Meanwhile, all we can do is attempt to change what we see in the future—and hope for the best.

Certainly all that has gone before in these Action Plans needs to be brought to bear in order to focus psychotronic energy in a laser-like beam for maximum power, especially *these:*

- Hooking up with the Cosmic Psychotronic Generator (Chapter 3)
- Increasing power through intent (Chapter 3)
- Enhancing results through geometric symbols (Chapter 5)
- Instant alpha relaxation (Chapter 6)
- Enlisting the support of unseen power (Chapter 7)
- Becoming space minded (Chapter 8)
- Cementing universal consciousness relations (Chapter 9)
- Phasing your psychotronic power with that of the universe (Chapter 11)
- Adding force to your commands with color (Chapter 11)

These are Action Plans which, when combined, intensify the

energy your consciousness produces, making positive thinking positively effective.

Remember, you have two great pieces of artillery with which to project this irrepressible energy—your eyes and your hands. Before attempting to change the future you need to prepare these two "applicators" for more efficient operation.

Action plan to "rev up" eyes and hands as psychotronic transmitters

Stare at your hands.

"See" them radiating energy.

Surround your hands with orange light.

Point your fingers at some object at the other side of the room.

Imagine the object heating up.

Stare at the object.

Imagine the object heating up even more with the combined hand and eye power.

Repeat several times before a future-changing Action Plan.

If you have . . .

- Accepted philosophically in your mind the possibility of a cause-effect "set" that prevents change
- Performed psychotronic power-enhancing Action Plans listed above
- "Revved-up" your hands and eyes as psychotronic generators

. . . you are ready to go to work.

Action plan to change the future

Go to your "special room."

Relax deeply.

Re-create the screen.

Adjust the perpetual calendar to the date in the future you previously saw involving events you wish to change.

Place a black frame around the screen.

Invite the unwanted events to play themselves once more on the screen.

Call your unseen universal forces for assistance.

Open the aperature of your eyes.

Extend your hands and point with both of your index fingers at the black frame.

Make it light up until it is a luminescent white.

Replay the scene as you wish it to be (see the good outcome generally rather than in specific ways).

Rest for a few moments with hands on lap, eyes closed, in a feeling of relief, gratitude, and acceptance.

You can use this Action Plan in matters involving individuals who are seen in your future-viewing to be acting in ways that are contrary to the common good. You have a good chance to change those ways for the benefit of yourself and others.

The smaller the group of people, the better the chance of seeing the desired change take place. This does not mean that large groups cannot be affected. They most certainly can. This work should be done even if an entire nation is involved. Obviously, though, your psychotronic energy, as powerful as it is, can make only a slight change in the outcome.

Do not hesitate because of this. The slight change will bring more psychotronic energy to bear toward the result. It will snowball. It will happen!

13

HOW TO KEEP PSYCHOTRONIC ENERGY WORKING FOR A FLOW OF RICHES THE REST OF YOUR LIFE

In this chapter you learn about some tools that are helpful to magnify your psychotronic power and what you can do in just a few minutes a day to keep up the flow of miracles in your life. You receive a simple technique to know somebody else's thoughts, another technique to make a change in your life, and finally a call to sound for greater universal psychotronic energy to renew your life.

Reba T. had some pet rabbits. One was acting strangely, hopping around in circles. Reba relaxed, went to her "special room," and imagined the rabbit there. She asked him what was wrong. Immediately the idea came to her that something was sticking him near his tail. She ended her Action Plan, went over to the cage, lifted out the rabbit, and examined him. Sure enough he had a large wood splinter there which she easily removed.

Compare this trivial matter with Roger B. Roger studied psychotronics and used it daily. He reaped benefits from every Action Plan. But then things went so well in his life, he found little need to use Action Plans. He traveled, lived well, and whenever some need arose, it seemed to get filled.

Reba was a psychotronic beginner. Roger was a psychotronic pro. In the first few chapters of this book, you learned to crawl. Subsequent Action Plans increased your psychotronic skills. You are about to become a pro.

If you are using the Action Plan in this book to change your life, you are approaching a point where the step-by-step processes they spell out are no longer necessary.

The mind adjusts to automatic use of psychotronic energy for the reasons you applied the Action Plans. You begin to sense the future; your will is supported by others; people behave properly with you and to you. Everything seems to go well. You wonder if you are really doing it. You are.

You were creating the obstacles others once threw at you. You were creating the money problems. You were your own worst enemy. Your energy of consciousness was negatively oriented with feelings of inferiority, persecution, lack, and lucklessness.

Being aware of your energy of consciousness—acquiring a knowledge of your psychotronic energy—is all that is necessary to change things around. That is one of the miracles of psychotronics. It is not like electrical energy where you have to make the necessary technical installations to utilize it.

You already have all the equipment. You just have to know how to use it.

When you begin to use it, it produces results. The more you use, the more miraculous the results, until you reach the point where, without half trying, the miracles of precognition, luck, love, and fortune become a way of life.

It is the ones who have not applied the Action Plans, the non-active readers, to whom I would like to address a few thoughts. There are some tools that might make you more comfortable working with psychotronic energy.

THE TOOLS THAT ARE BEING DEVISED TO HARNESS AND FOCUS PSYCHOTRONIC ENERGY

We have already discussed the use of divining rods and pendulums. These are used to amplify the sensing of psychotronic vibrations through our brain and nervous system—a process known as radiesthesia.

Psychotronic energy from the Cosmic Psychotronic Generator was harnessed thousands of years ago by the Egyptians. Egyptian culture is now recognized to be centered around this sensing. The story of Moses and how his rod turned into a snake and devoured the snake of the priests is symbolic talk for Moses being able to out-divine the Egyptian diviners.

Today the pyramids are recognized as a focusing device for Cosmic Psychotronic Energy. One modern young scientist, Pat Flanagan, has made the miniature pyramid a popular meditation tool. However, the research continues beyond this usage.

Egyptian priests first used the psychotronic power of their pyramids to prevent decay. Today experiments are being carried out that point to the magnification as well as the arresting of life energy within us by use of the pyramid shape.

Wilhelm Reich in this century attempted to capture what he called "orgone" energy with a specially made box. His work was controversial then but is being re-examined today.

Perhaps the man who is doing the most in the field of research into psychotronic devices is Christopher Hills, director of the University of the Trees in Boulder Creek, California. He has combined the pendulum and pyramid principles to create a psychotronic power detector. The Hills Positive Green Pendulum is tuned to the same positive life-giving energy that comes off the top of the capstone of a pyramid. The center of the pendulum contains radioactive power. The pendulum reacts clockwise when there is life-energy within food plants, counterclockwise when the plants contain disease and disintegrating energy or agents.

Hills has also devised pendulums for use over water tables to detect whether they are health-giving or not, and pendulums that are magnet-fitted to confirm whether your insight into someone else's thoughts are correct. A plain wood pendulum can be used to recharge the body and change negative emotions to positive.

The Hills Pi-Ray Orgone Accumulation is a small wooden box, specially constructed, with a metallic coil. It purportedly adds zest and energy when a person's photo is placed within. The box acts as a lens that focuses Cosmic Psychotronic Energy.

I asked Christopher Hills for an instance of when this box worked. He said that it had worked in his own life just a short time previously. His son John had broken his toe. His wife Norah decided to use the box to accelerate healing. She placed a photo of John in the box taken when his toe was perfect. For good measure, she wrote $1,000 on a piece of paper and put that in also.

Three days later the toe was healed. Also, a man arrived who asked John if he could do a cover photo for his magazine, a new but growing one. John refused saying "I'd like to but I'm short of cash and need to spend my time on projects that will make me some money." With that the man reached into his wallet and pulled out a thousand dollars.

"Here's an advance," he said.

HOW TO MAKE YOUR OWN PSYCHOTRONIC "MONEY MACHINE"

You can use a small wooden box as a tool to make your psychotronic energy work more precisely for you. Here is how.

Action plan to create a psychotronic money machine

Understand that you will start with a small wood jewelry box, and that you will need to be "led" to just the right box.

Test each small box you have by holding a pendulum over it and asking the question, "Is this the right box for my psychotronic money machine?"

Pick the box that gives the pendulum the greatest movement or agitation.

Place and glue down a tiny piece of gold in the box, even if only a small link of gold-plated chain.

Sleep with this box under your pillow for at least a week and take it wherever you go during the daytime, keeping it as close to your person as possible, in the car, in your hand or shoulder bag or other private spot.

Go to your "special room" after the week is over, holding the box in your hand.

See light from the skylight going into the top of your head, down your body and out of your solar plexus onto the box.

Charge the box in this manner for three minutes.

End your session.

Here is how to use this box as a money machine.

1. Write down on a piece of paper any money need you have, such as "I need $5,000 to buy a new car."
2. Fold the piece of paper with the writing on the inside and place the paper in the psychotronic money machine.
3. Place the box in a safe but visible place—such as in your living room on a book shelf or window sill.
4. Know that the machine is already at work.
5. When you receive the money, you can refill the box with your next "order" for money.

Dorothy H. was a divorcee. She had two teenagers to care for and not enough income from her ex, so she decided to go back to her old career as a vocalist. But bookings take time and she had started to borrow money from friends to pay her bills. One friend helped her make a psychotronic money machine. Her first order was for $1,000 a week. Within five days she received an offer to act as social hostess at a hotel and to sing in the evening at their dining room. The salary offered was $1,000 a week. Now, thanks to her psychotronic money machine, she is always in demand and money is plentiful.

If you need a tool to relate to broader consciousness, there are of course religious objects available as well as a wide selection of amulets, charms and talismans, the presence of which on or near your person have that desired effect.

Their promise is to the skeptical, rather than to the believer. But in this step of evolution—the step called psychotronics, where miracles are the order of the day—skeptics are in the majority, so the promise of these devices is a useful one.

If you have not been performing the Action Plans, it is never too late to start. I recommend that you consider a tool.

The most common tools are tools to relax—metronones, vocal tapes that induce progressive relaxation, music tapes or records that induce tranquility, and others. These are useful for those to whom relaxation is the problem.

However, motivation and belief seem to be the more imposing problems. These require uncommon tools, such as the few I have described.

ABOUT PSYCHOTRONIC COURSES AND THEIR POSSIBLE VALUE TO YOU AS A TOOL

A cover of *Newsweek* magazine (issue of September 6, 1976) showed a man's head with a number of labels on it including Bioenergetics, TM, est, Silva Mind Control, Psychosynthesis, Arica, and Rolfing.

The title was "Getting Your Head Together," and the story in this issue covered the ways that these courses or programs helped you to grow and move ahead. I have had exposure to all of these programs and many more. They are all good depending on your needs and stage of growth. If I had to recommend one it would be Silva Mind Control.

One of the most startling developments of the century has been happening quietly in hired halls and hotel meeting rooms throughout the country. Men and women in all walks of life are discovering they have a mental ability they never knew they had. In some 48 hours of experience, they are able to demonstrate to their own amazement that they can sense accurately hundreds of miles away and detect important information. They are learning to visualize in a special way and make it happen. There are now seven million graduates in North and South America and Europe.

I have gone through the Silva Mind Control experience several times with different lecturers. I have taken the graduate lecture series from Jose Silva and repeated it twice with top Silva Mind Control staffers. I have helped to train others. But best of all, I have had the privilege of using the mental training for three years in my own life. I can vouch for the fact that everything you hear about this training is as miraculous as it sounds.

Ordinary people like you and me become extraordinary people before the week of training is over, able to correct health problems, create wealth, and move steadily toward whatever goal we set.

Use tools, read books, take courses—they all help you to become a superhuman with super-brainpower as your psychotronic energy of consciousness begins to flow.

THE ONE DAILY STEP THAT KEEPS PSYCHOTRONIC ENERGY FLOWING THROUGH YOU

Rudy J. is a successful jewelry designer. However, a few years ago things were not going well. His designs were not receiving acceptance. They were original, maybe too original. Customers would look, approve, but then walk away. Rudy had to take a part time job as a salesman in a jewelry store to make ends meet.

Rudy understood creativity. He saw it as his own psychotronic energy performing in a special way. He realized that this way needed to be more in tune with the demands—with the tastes and desires of other people. He realized his psychotronic energy was not fully "in phase" with theirs.

So he decided to do something about it. A special room in his imagination where he could attune his consciousness to universal consciousness was fine, but he decided that by creating a real room—skylight and all—he could both attune and design there. He built the room—a type of meditation sanctuary—a place where he could reinforce his connection with the Cosmic Psychotronic Generator daily and then work with metals and jewels in greater attunement. He went into this room and sat quietly each day before getting to work.

Within several weeks Rudy J. began to see a difference in his own work. Instead of original designs of an artistic nature that another person might find interesting but nothing more, his designs began to take on a more symbolic, spiritual significance. Serpents, circles, crosses and other symbols combined with the heads of Biblical characters and those from other books of wisdom became the features of his jewelry.

People admired and bought. He became the private jeweler for several diplomats and influential people. He became the successful jewelry designer he is today.

If there is only one act that you can do to improve your life, that act would be to spend a few minutes a day as Rudy J. did. You do not need an actual place in your house to relax and turn your consciousness to the universe. You can imagine you are in such a room.

Read Action Plans in Chapter 2 again and decide you will start with these. Then do this Action Plan daily.

Daily action plan for continuing power

Spend a few minutes in your special room, relaxed, and just sensing the greater consciousness that surrounds yours—the source of psychotronic energy that hooks in and gives you crackling mental energy the moment you think of it.

Know that you are not being strange when you do this. Millions are now doing it secretly. Indeed, you are being left behind by not doing it.

In a village near Bologna, Italy, a ten year old boy happened to watch Uri Geller bend keys and forks on a television show. Now, Paride Giatt has gone on television himself to demonstrate his psychotronic power to millions of Italian viewers.

Dr. Massimo Inardi, a physician and president of the Center for Parapsychology in Bologna, was quoted in the National Enquirer as predicting that in time Paride could become better at bending metal with the powers of his mind than even Uri.

A New York woman heard about a Moscow woman who could move objects across a table mentally. She said that if a Russian woman could do it, she could do it. And within several months of practice, she too was doing it.

Tokyo grade school boys heard about mental powers used to bend forks. They are doing it.

You have now heard about psychotronic power to bring money, power, control, love and luck. Why not make the decision to join those who are using it and improving their life?

THE MOST ADVANCED PSYCHOTRONIC MIRACLE OF ALL

I would now like to get back to you who have made the decision and have been working miracles already in your life, using the Action Plans in the preceding chapters.

Psychotronics is a new science. Its incredible results today will be looked on tomorrow as run of the mill. You and I probably cannot conceive of, much less believe, the kinds of miracles that may be within the realm of human accomplishment a few years from now.

About the furthest my own consciousness can go now in accepting these miracles is the act of *getting into somebody else's consciousness.* That to me is the ultimate.

It is easier for me to conceive of universal consciousness interceding in a tidal wave or earthquake, or of individual consciousness, tapping the future and changing it, than it is for me to conceive of "putting on somebody's head" and feeling and knowing that person's attitudes, emotions and intentions. Still, I have done it and others have done it. And you are going to do it now.

First, a word of caution. Your own head is often uncomfortable to you. Something worries you, gnaws at you, "bugs" you. If another person "put on your head," that person would feel even more uncomfortable than you do. You have already adjusted to your own thoughts and feelings no matter how ill at ease you are. Another person can find them a decided shock. When you "put on somebody's head" do so cautiously, ready to detect what you need to and then "take it off" rapidly.

What is meant by "putting on somebody's head?" This is purely an imaginary act but remember we are dealing with the energy of consciousness and so the imaginary act has a very real effect. The intent of "putting on somebody's head" is to penetrate the thoughts and feelings of that person–to get into his or her "space."

Vivian L. needed my help. I agreed to a friendly "counseling" session. We talked for a half hour. Vivian spoke of her unhappiness. Her apartment was too small. Her job did not pay enough. But I sensed there was more behind the depression she seemed to be going through than she was telling me about.

I decided to end the session abruptly on the excuse that I had another appointment. We set another session for the next day. As soon as she left, I went to my "special room" under the skylight, put Vivian on my imaginary screen, took her head off, and turning it around placed it on my own head like a helmet.

Immediately, I felt what was lacking. She was lonely. She had a boy friend. But he was not fulfilling her sexual needs. I recalled her experience the last time with him–there was no climax on her part.

I "took her head off," as everything seemed explained now.

When Vivian returned the next day, I went right to her love life. Who is your boy friend? What does he mean to you? Net result–I recommended that the two of them visit a marriage counselor even though they were not thinking in those terms–for sexual techniques.

A month later I happened to see Vivian again. She was radiant. She shared no details about her love life, but neither did she have any problems to unload.

You can use the Action Plan that follows to:

- Know what a competitor is planning
- Feel physical symptoms that another person is experiencing
- Foresee where another person plans to go or with whom
- Pick up inner thoughts of another about you or about somebody else
- Identify attitudes or emotions to predict what otherwise might be unpredictable behavior

You cannot use the Action Plan that follows to:

- Create a problem for somebody you do not like
- Sabotage somebody's thoughts
- Hurt somebody through another person

If you decide to use this Action Plan for this type of interference with others, it may appear to work but this is the missile merely hitting the target in order to return its mission of hurt to the sender.

Action plan to get inside another person's head

Go to your "special room" under the skylight.

Activate your screen.

Make the person whose thoughts or feelings you wish to detect appear on your screen.

Magnify the image so that the head fills the screen.

Move the magnified image closer to you, seeing it get still bigger.

Turn the person around so that the back of the head is now facing you.

Reach your hands forward and place one on each side of the person's head.

Put the head on yours as if it were a helmet. (Should there be an acute feeling of discomfort, merely remove the head and return it to the screen. Try again later that day or the next day.)

Observe your own thoughts, feelings, bodily pains or sensations as these are the predominant thoughts and feelings of that person.

Ask a question about what you wish to know if you have not already detected the answer.

Accept the thoughts that come as quite likely the person's thoughts even though they appear to be phantasy or guessing on your part.

Return the head to the screen.

Turn the person around to again see the face.

Send positive thoughts of understanding and oneness.

Make the person disappear from your screen and end your session.

We have good reason to believe that the scientists of some countries have been able to control an individual's mind at a distance. This control can be in the nature of distorting what is seen into what the controller wants the controlled to see. It is suspected that some method analogous to the above Action Plan is being used. So far, we know no shield against this.

Apparently, nature provides for a sharing of consciousness, as it is basically all part of the universal consciousness. But nature also provides for a return to the perpetrator of any evil perpetrated.

HOW TO CHANGE THE WORLD AROUND YOU AND MAKE IT A BETTER WORLD FOR YOU TO LIVE IN

The author studied many years ago with a wise philosopher, Dr. Jacques Bustanoby, a Basque who had a center in New Jersey. Often, students volunteered to help with improvements at the center.

One afternoon I telephoned to say that I would be over later to help with the exterior painting of the building. "But don't assign me to the fourth story," I implored. "I am not that good on a ladder."

"Fine," he replied, "Why don't you plan on staying for dinner?" When I agreed, he asked if there was anything I could not eat. "I can eat everything," I assured him, "except liver does not agree with me."

When I arrived a couple of hours later, I was given a brush and a paint can and ushered to a ladder at the rear of the building. "That dormer on the fourth floor is what I'd like you to complete," said Dr. Bustanoby, pointing skyward.

With my heart in my mouth, I climbed slowly up, without

looking down, and began to paint, occupying my mind with the lesson he was giving me.

Later, I was rewarded with a delicious dinner—calf's liver and onions.

The two-pronged lesson was without words. Perhaps that is why it was so clear:

We manufacture our own prison walls. Some live their entire life a prisoner within these fears, suspicions, anxieties, and other negative uses of the energy of consciousness. Others are fortunate enough to meet a wise man who whispers in their ear. They try the prison door, and find that it was never locked. I can climb ladders now. And I love liver.

Dr. Norman Vincent Peale never used the word "psychotronics" in his famous book, *The Power of Positive Thinking.* That book sold in the millions and changed many a life. What power does positive thinking tap? When your doctorate is in religion, it is natural for you to see that power as the power of God. When your doctorate is in physics, it is natural for you to see that power as the power of psychotronics.

Is your life a funeral dirge or a song of victory? If you do not like the tune, you can change it. You now have an easy way to make any change you want in your life: *Just push the right psychotronic button.*

In electricity, you have to read the electrical diagram to know what any particular switch or button will do. In psychotronics all you need to do is desire it, knowing that desiring it automatically places your power in resonance with the wavelength necessary to accomplish the desire.

Right now, you need a methodology to implement this desire—an Action Plan. After you have performed scores of Action Plans, the desire and positive visualizing is all that you need—no methodology, no going to an imaginary meditation room under a skylight to the universe, no conscious relaxing, no screen. You will be able to walk along the sidewalk, "see" something happen where you are going that will make life better for you, and it is done. Meanwhile, though, you need to train your brain to function in this manner. That is the purpose of the Action Plan.

The basic Action Plan to make life better is as follows:

Action plan to change the world around you

Go to your special room under the skylight.

Create your screen.

See yourself on the screen as you are, with other people if they are involved, in ways that you are not happy or satisfied with.

Light up the frame of the screen.

Change the picture of you to the way you wish it to be, people and circumstances changing, too.

Dwell for a few minutes in this positive picture.

End your session, knowing that psychotronic energy is already at work making it so.

John J. was a brilliant thinker, but he was always broke. For some strange reason, he was never able to take a good idea–like his idea for a Chinese buffet, his idea for a book on parties, his idea for a modeling school and agency–and bring them into fruition. His friends looked at John as "all talk and no action."

Then John began studying psychotronics. It seemed it was something he already knew–it really struck home. And what struck home hardest was his own psychotronic error: He was talking about his creative ideas and short-circuiting his psychotronic energy. He stopped talking and started going to his "special room" under the skylight where he saw himself creating his latest idea and the right people coming to help him. Soon he had a "swap meet" going, a health food vending truck, and he was writing novelty greeting cards. Money was coming in from many directions–and it was just the beginning for the now wealthy John.

How many thoughts are there in this world? The number is astronomical and increasing every moment. Every thought, repeated with any constancy, is created in the physical world. This is understood when we watch the sculptor at work, or the architect, or the interior designer. But this thought-to-matter process is working constantly. All the good things we live with are thought-created. And all the bad.

Man's inhumanity to man makes the front pages. Fires, wars, collisions, crashes, deaths, diseases make the front pages. The good things are on the back pages–if in print at all. The violence, the oppression, the crime, and the strife occupy our attention many times more intensely than do the awards, good deeds, successes. These things challenge any belief we might have there is a beneficent God, or that man is good, or that life is meant to be joyous. We begin to see life as painful, tragic, a "vale of tears."

So we are giving more creative energy to these negative happenings, more psychotronic power. And we are learning more vividly every day that life is bad. Is this the lesson we want to learn? If so, then go ahead and learn it. The rest of you follow me.

The lesson I teach, and which I am learning more and more every day I live, is that the choice is ours and that the life we choose can be one of joy, fulfillment, creative invention, power, fame, respect, health, longevity and good. Choose this life and you begin to get the sneaking suspicion that this is one that has been meant for you to have right along.

A SOUND YOU CAN USE FOR A SOUND LIFE

A three-year study made at the Medical Institute of Benares Hindu University has, in the words of its director, Dr. K. N. Udupa, concluded that yoga and meditation can be good for you. In a country where the people have been practicing yoga and meditation for centuries to make this study is somewhat of a paradox. While Yoga and meditation has spread to the West, the present generation in India has drifted away from it.

Now they are rediscovering its ability to relieve stressful diseases of modern living such as insomnia, drug addiction, ulcers, and heart trouble. It is also seen to increase virility and to slow aging, help in weight control, lower blood pressure, and relieve respiratory problems. The Action Plans dictated by the science of psychotronics are quite analogous to types of yoga and meditation.

We are also rediscovering the ancient wisdom about the pyramid shape and how it helps to focus energy analogous to what we tap into with consciousness from the Cosmic Psychotronic Generator. Mariner 9 photographs taken in 1972 show formations strikingly like Egyptian pyramids sitting on a flat plain–perfect tetrahedrons.

The Action Plans dictated by the science of psychotronics are quite analogous to sitting in a special place where the energy is focused.

In a moment this book is going to end. But for you it is just the beginning. You are not only making your life better in many ways, you are making this world a better one to live in for everybody. Here is a tool. It is a built-in tool that you can use to excite your psychotronic energy and resonate it with your universal flow of psychotronic energy. It is your voice.

All energy is vibration. If you use your voice, you create vibrations. Whenever you use your voice, you are producing either negative or positive energy, energy that is either destructive or creative. You help your own consciousness when you use your voice for positive words rather than negative words. Your psychotronic energy works for you when you say, "Every day, in every way I am getting better and better." It works just as obediently *against* you, should you use your voice to say, "Every day, in every way I am getting worse and worse."

One of the most creative sounds you can utter with your voice has been used by yogis in India for centuries. It is a sound which you can spell as "OM" or AUM." It is pronounced like "home" only without the "h." It is the closest the human voice can come to the sound of the universe—defined as the total sounds of the atoms, molecules, planets, and galaxies. When you sound Om, everything resonates to this sound. You can "hear" it with a tingling of your own palms if you hold your arms out, palms down.

I am going to ask you to sound it, though, with your palms up in a receiving posture. Then, after sounding OM, your hands will feel energized and your eyes will be better transmitters of psychotronic power.

Ready? Then begin . . .

Action plan to sound the call for universal energy

Relax in a seated position.

Place hands on lap, palms up.

Close eyes.

Intone OM in a monotone manner, holding the M sound as long as your breath holds out.

Repeat two more times.

Remain with eyes closed in seated position for a minute or so.

Be conscious of the universe you are part of.

Love the universe.

End your session, but . . . .

Begin a new life!